1978

ALBERT CAMUS:

The Invincible Summer

ALBERT CAMUS:

The Invincible Summer

BY ALBERT MAQUET

From the French
"Albert Camus ou l'Invincible Eté"

New York
HUMANITIES PRESS
1972

Reprinted by Humanities Press
1972 by arrangement with
the British publisher

© John Calder (Publishers) Ltd. 1958
Originally published in Paris by
Nouvelle Editions Debresse à Paris

SBN-391-00269-4

Printed in the United States of America

*In the midst of winter, I finally
learned that there was in me
an invincible summer.*

—CAMUS, IN *L'Eté*

AUTHOR'S NOTE

The work of Albert Camus is of the kind that requires us to be worthy of it.

At the very least, we are expected to respond to the honesty of its message by the honesty of our reading.

Our present essay was conceived with this scrupulous intention and with the hope of sharing it.

We have therefore devoted ourselves to describing as faithfully as possible the double experiment, lyrical and intellectual, of the author, and to showing the stages of evolution that become apparent.

—A.M.

CONTENTS

Contents

Part i.

THE MAN AND

HIS STRUGGLES

i.

THE MAN AND
HIS STRUGGLES

> In Albert Camus one senses a patient and deliberate lucidity, but at the same time something else: a restrained energy—and a fierce rage to live, which scorns feverishness but which will suffer no delay.
>
> GAËTAN PICON,
> *Le Littéraire*, Aug. 10, 1946.

1. THE NORTH AFRICAN

Albert Camus was born on November 7, 1913, at Mondovi, the county seat of the department of Constantine, beneath the privileged skies of Algeria. He was born, he tells us, "in a land of plenty on the shores of a happy sea." Not for nothing is a man the elect of sun and beauty: in the prodigious shimmering of the light, the soul is gorged with the pride of living. "Sea, plain, silence, perfumes of that land! I filled myself with a fragrant life, and I bit into the already sun-gilded fruit of the world, overwhelmed as I felt its strong, sweet juices trickle from my lips. No, it was not I that counted, nor the world, but only the harmony and the silence which made love spring up between us."[1]

Thus, from the moment he opened his eyes as a child, a certain quality of light consummated his "nuptials" with the land, a land of opulence and of destitution, where the flesh consumes its treasures in the burning impatience of existence, where the mind seeks its truth in its own negation. Implacable and generous land, land "without lessons," he tells us, in *Noces*. "Its pleasures have no remedy, and its joys remain without hope. What it demands are clairvoyant souls, that is to say, souls without consolation. It requires us to make an act of lucidity as one makes an act of faith. Singular country, that bestows simultaneously upon the man it nurtures its splendor along with its misery!"[2]

Singular situation for the child who was to be deprived of the ordinary things of life while his senses were daily overwhelmed by the abundance of nature! Camus, the son of a humble farm laborer who was killed

[1] *Noces*, p. 29, *nouvelle édition*, Charlot, 1945.
[2] *Noces*, pp. 54-55.

14

in 1914 at the first Battle of the Marne, was to comprehend quite soon the hard reality of his condition.

On the one hand, there was the divine voluptuousness of a banquet over which the sun presided, a voluptuousness pregnant with a terrible truth—"Everything that exalts life increases, at the same time, its absurdity." On the other hand, there was the bondage to which the destitute are reduced by social injustice. But on every side, humiliation. Later on, Camus was to revolt against the absurd, and open his heart to sympathy.

However, to lose sight of the fact that this revolt, far from germinating in the stony soil of bitterness, matured on the very slopes of plenty, is to risk betraying the man and understanding nothing of the writer. "I may have had my share of hardships," he confided to G. d'Abuarède one day,[3] "but I did not begin my life as a rebel, and by the same token I did not begin my literary life with imprecation or disparagement, as some writers do, but with admiration."

His character as a youth was to be forged in the crucible of study, athletic sports, and poverty. After primary and secondary schools, he studied philosophy at the Faculté des Lettres of the University of Algiers, where he obtained his Master's degree by presenting a thesis on Plotinus and St. Augustine.

[3] *Les Nouvelles Littéraires*, May 10, 1951.

But the discipline of the classroom did not banish the sports stadium from his mind. "The African University," Camus remarked in a letter to a friend,[4] "differs from its French counterparts by resembling much more—both as to the natural setting and the way of life—the colleges of the Stoics than it does the prison-like colleges of the metropolis." And he adds: "Our greatest occupation was—and for a long time remained so for me—athletics. It was on the playing fields that I learned my only lessons in moral ethics."

But still another lesson awaited him: that which life reserves for the poverty-stricken student. Necessity was to compel him to divide his time between studies and paid employment. He was successively automobile accessories salesman, ship broker, meteorologist, and clerk at police headquarters. Thus he learned, in different fields of activity, the dull routine of the workingman's existence. But he also learned the obscure virtues which this uniformity, though it may submerge the worker, does not succeed in stifling in him.

Studies, sports, poverty filled his life. To this was to be added the ordeal of a long illness that laid him low while he was studying for his final examination in phi-

[4] Extract from a letter quoted by P. Néraud de Boisdeffre, in "Albert Camus, ou l'expérience tragique," in *Etudes,* December, 1950, pp. 303-304.

losophy. It is not to be wondered at that a man whose will was thus tempered felt obliged one day to raise his voice, and in a message of grandeur.

But, until world events drew him out of himself, nothing yet concerned him but to serve art. Passionately fond of the theatre, Camus organized, with a few friends, an acting group which he directed. Its very name, *L'Equipe*—The Working Gang—describes it. After having produced an adaptation of Malraux's *Le Temps de Mépris*, the company staged an original four-act play, *Révolte dans les Asturies*,[5] which was directly inspired by the uprising of the Oviedo miners. The play had the honor of being suppressed by the Government of Algeria. Camus next produced *Le Paquebot "Tenacity"*, by Vildrac, Ben Jonson's *Silent Woman*, Dostoyevsky's *The Brothers Karamazov*, in which he played the part of Ivan, his own adaptation of Aeschylus' *Prometheus*, which still remains unpublished, Pushkin's *Don Juan*, and versions of Gide's *Le Retour de l'Enfant prodigue* and Gorki's *Bas-Fonds*.

Camus followed up the theatrical venture with the adventure of travel, visiting Italy, Austria, Prague, the Balearic Isles, in one of those parentheses of life, a time

---

[5] Although a collective work, this four-act play cannot conceal the amount it owes to the young Camus. It was published in 1936 by Edm. Charlot, "Pour les Amis du Théâtre du travail," in Algiers.

when the mind, relaxed, on vacation, makes itself as it were porous, open to the discovery of verities only afforded by utterly new and foreign surroundings.

To serve art was his sole aim. To be convinced of the sincerity of this program, one has only to read the two little essays the then unknown young man published at the time, *L'Envers et L'Endroit,* and *Noces*—a privilege granted to but a few, since the publications were in small printings. That there were already in these early works certain evidences of deeper preoccupations is something that can now be seen only too clearly. At the time, no one noticed them—or at any rate, very few—for Camus was so young.[6]

2. THE JOURNALIST AND RESISTANT

He was twenty-five, and doubtless, like every ephebus of the Mediterranean beaches, had "an eagerness to live that was almost prodigious." Journalism began to engross him. After some practice skirmishes on the Algiers *Républicain,* he went, in 1940, to Paris. He did some work on the important evening newspaper, *Paris-Soir,* but quit in June of the same year. He found himself with time to begin work on his novel, *L'Etranger.* By 1941

[6] No one noticed it but Henry de Montherlant who was then living in Tunis; from there he addressed a letter of praise to the author. (Cf. the article by M. Muller in *Carrefour,* December 20, 1949.)

he was back again in Algiers. But he fell ill and was forced to return, the following year, to a France that was now engulfed in war.

The hour of the Resistance, the hour of the voyage to the end of night and of the "battle of shadows" had come. Camus did his fighting with the team that edited the clandestine newspaper *Combat,* and was soon in the hurly-burly of those working for the Liberation, ranging from Lyons to Paris at the side of his friend, Leynaud, who was later to be arrested and shot by the enemy. "By his very function, the artist is a witness for liberty, and it is a justification for which he sometimes has to pay dearly."[7] His *"engagement"* is therefore but an act of simple fidelity to his vocation: ". . . it is not the combat which makes artists out of us, but art which compels us to be combatants."[8]

Immediately after the war, Camus took over the direction of the newspaper *Combat,* and the movement for which it stood. The brilliant editorials that he published—unsigned—contributed a great deal to the popularity of *Combat* with intellectuals. Nevertheless he soon withdrew from the mêlée, even if he carried away from that harrowing commitment less of rancor than a fierce hope. Returning to the newspaper in 1946,

[7] and [8] *Actuelles,* Chroniques (1944-1948), p. 264. Paris, Gallimard, 1950.

he abandoned it definitely in 1947, handing over the editorship to Claude Bourdet. He withdrew from public affairs, but not at all in bitterness: his convictions had gained in strength what they had lost in illusions. As he stated much later,[9] "For two years we ran an absolutely independent newspaper which nothing ever compromised. I ask no more. Everything, at one time or another, bears fruit."

The journalist, at the age of thirty-two, was restored to himself, with his burning passion for justice, his violent hunger for fraternity, and with his artist's vocation. Behind him, he had left many markers along the path that led from the Maquis to the political arena: in 1942 the novel *L'Etranger* and the essays *Le Mythe de Sisyphe*, in 1944 the plays *Le Malentendu* and *Caligula*, and the collection of letters *Lettres à un Ami allemand*, which were published as a book in 1945.

3. THE MILITANT

From then on, the defense of human values towered so hugely in Camus' attention that biographical anecdote vanishes, as if absorbed in the pure fire of a crusade in which, silhouetted against the "deepest gloom," the face of the thinker and the thought he thinks become indistinguishable.

[9] In the magazine *Caliban*, no. 54, August 1951, p. 16.

After a lecture tour in America (1946), Camus returned to the world of myth and, in defense of man and human happiness, testified once more against the epoch and against history. In June 1947 he published *La Peste*. One reviewer hailed the book as "a manifesto, in the second post-war period, of antiterrorism, a manifesto with social significance that may be considerable twenty years from now."[10]

Now, however reluctantly, the tone of the writer grew harsher. Faced with a political world that seemed to have forgotten the past, and was again in deadlock, Camus denounced, with every energy he commanded, the monstrous aberration of this historical logic. In the name of ideologies, he tells us, man divides against man, damning all of us to a lonely hell if we will not choose the one thing that can save us. We must face what is happening, we must not destroy ourselves. He pleads for the free exchange of words and ideas among all men *("le dialogue et la communication universelle des hommes entre eux")* as the antidote to the atom bomb. This is the burden of *Ni victimes ni bourreaux*, the virile articles of November 1948: "Since the experiment that controls the fate of the whole world goes on, and since it is inevitable that it will go still further, it is not a bad thing for men to think of preserving, through the apoca-

[10] Bernard d'Astorg, in *Esprit*, October 1947, p. 621.

lyptic history that awaits us, the humble right to think, which, without any pretense of solving everything, will nonetheless be ready at every moment to give some meaning to everyday life."[11]

The essayist pursues and maintains this thought, but it remained for the playwright to make it flash out in all its tragic clarity. *L'Etat de Siège* is the dramatic ceremony of Camus' irrevocable break with the "contemporary political society" that he had found wallowing in compromise, corrupted with lies, and, finally, despicable. Such an attitude, we must note, is neither facile resignation nor withdrawal. Rather, it enlists the individual in a struggle that is all the more intense because it is on the side of life, that is all the more noble and irresistible because it is armed against death only with intelligence and human sympathy, that seeks what is still worth seeking: to *save lives*. In disengaging oneself from public action to preserve one's integrity, the conscience cannot but have a feeling of disgust; but immediately love of humanity intervenes, fecundating the revolt, orienting it towards private action: "The world in which I live is repugnant, but I feel myself one with the human beings who suffer in it. There are some ambitions which are not mine and I would feel ill at ease if I were to make my way by depending upon

[11] *Actuelles*, p. 178.

the poor privileges that are reserved for those who accommodate themselves to this society. But it seems to me there is another ambition which should be that of all writers: to bear witness and shout, each time it is possible, and according to our ability, for those who, like us, are enslaved."[12]

4. THE REBEL

Again it was in the theatre, this time with the play *Les Justes* (1949) that this cry echoed. Torn from oblivion for a moment and for our edification, that handful of Russian terrorists of the beginning of the century come, in this play, to reaffirm, while being torn by inner contradictions, the moral demands of all rebellion and the price they consented to pay so that theirs might conserve its original purity. A veritable cry of alarm before the excesses of our time: ". . . If the only solution is death, then we are not on the right track. The right track is the one that leads to life, to the sunlight. One cannot unceasingly suffer from cold."

Nor can one unceasingly shout. There comes a time when, while proceeding along the path from the historical experience which begot it towards the attitude it seeks to inspire in order to dominate history, the mind is aroused to renew contact with itself, to collect its

[12] *Actuelles,* pp. 249-250.

thoughts, and to confront itself. After bearing witness, there comes a time for a new kind of thinking, a broadening and shading of thoughts. This will be found in *L'Homme Révolté,* a collection of essays published in 1951, the fruit of a four year period of such thinking on Camus' part, in which his thought, shot through with an intense hope, attains its plenitude. From the depths of the inhuman night where his revolt first manifested itself, Camus has achieved, in this book of essays, the serene realm of moderation; the revolt has become "pure tension," halfway between those who surrender themselves to God and those who deify man. Camus' revolt "gives without delay its force of love and refuses injustice without delay." This revolt, self-conquered, enables Camus to perceive at the end of the other night, whither the blind world turns, a light that is "inevitable . . . and for which we have but to struggle in order to make it shine."

Hope. *L'Espoir.* That is also the name of a series of books which Camus edits today in the publishing house of Gallimard.

Taking a stand against the contemporary nihilisms, both bourgeois and Marxist, *L'Homme Révolté* could not but arouse some disturbances in the press and public opinion.

In truth, although the book was much talked about,

people often talked about it after having read it carelessly. Which explains why the author felt obliged to intervene several times to rehabilitate his falsified theses.[13]

But also to be reckoned with were those who had not waited for this copious essay to form an opinion on the revolt: André Breton headed this rank, having opened fire upon the author after having read a chapter devoted to Lautréamont which appeared in the *Cahiers du Sud,* and having read it before it had been published. Camus replied. Thus, the controversy preceded the simple restatements of the argument, instead of rightly crowning them.

An important and insinuating article by Francis Jeanson set the argument in motion.[14] Invited to avail himself of his right to reply, Camus felt called upon to emerge from his habitual reserve, and addressed a letter of the same length and scope, in a stingingly indignant tone, to the editor of the magazine, who happened to be Jean-Paul Sartre. Called to account, Sartre contrived, with ferocious verve, to maltreat his colleague, though

---

[13] All the texts concerning this "combat" of Camus with his critics have been collected, along with others, in *Actuelles II,* Chroniques 1948-1953. Paris, Gallimard, 1953.

[14] Jeanson's article, entitled, *"Albert Camus ou l'âme révoltée",* appeared in *Temps Modernes,* May, 1952. The August number of the magazine groups together Camus' reply, Sartre's retort, and a final word from Jeanson himself, entitled, *"Pour tout vous dire . . ."*

25

he swore at the start of his diatribe that he would regret ever to lose Camus' friendship. This passage of arms caused an uproar, and pleased only the personal enemies of the debaters. Yet a clear understanding was needed where these two great minds were concerned. If some have come to regret that, in its bitterness, the argument ended in a breach of friendship, no one, Camus least of all, can be sorry that the truth was thus sifted and refined.

Part ii.

THE WRITER
AND THINKER

ii.

THE WRITER
AND THINKER

As with all great artists, he is at the same time
creator of works on the plane of art and custo-
dian of a doctrine of life on the plane of ethics.

ROBERT KANTERS,
La Gazette des Lettres, No. 28, June 1947.

Camus' work established itself among us suddenly, with
the weight and authority of a revelation. It forceably
set us in a moment of lucidity which glaringly showed
up our contradictions and the urgent need to remove
them. "As for me, confronting this society," the young
essayist exclaimed very early in his career, "I do not
want to lie, nor have people lie to me." This avowed
intention of intellectual asceticism, so jealously main-

29

tained in one book after another and, be it noted, unanimously hailed by the critics, had as its first effect the placing of his thought beyond reach of any system. Thus, from *L'Etranger* to *La Peste,* from *Le Mythe de Sisyphe* to *L'Homme Révolté,* we can follow the traces of a tension which has attained that point of intimate vibration in which his demands for justice and brotherly love reach a point of equilibrium.

In the period of activity represented by these works, several phases can, then, be recognized. To single them out is to discover at the same time their harmonic progression, the suddenly decisive echoes to old, secret calls. This thought-on-the-move was in fact foretokened by the author himself in *Le Mythe de Sisyphe:* ". . . the unique creation of a man is fortified in the successive and multiple aspects that are his works, which complete, correct, overtake, or even contradict each other."[15]

A. THE CONCEPT OF THE ABSURD, POINT OF DEPARTURE FOR THE THOUGHT

1. MAN'S PRESENCE IN THE WORLD

The first two essays written by Camus are a kind of lyrical prelude to his thought. He situates man at the very centre of the world spectacle and registers the

[15] *Le Mythe de Sisyphe,* pp. 154-155, new edition, Paris, 1945.

strange music which penetrates him progressively as his presence there endures. It is a music of discordant tonalities, since it simultaneously expresses happiness and bitterness.

The writer had by that time experienced life, had travelled sufficiently for his consciousness to be uprooted. *L'Envers et l'Endroit*[16] discloses traces of that first "shedding" of the past. (The *dénuement,* as the author calls it.) In this album of souvenirs, Prague and Palma de Majorca, Vienna and Venice, and Florence, symbolically mark the stages of a more profound journey, that of the soul.

As the humdrum daily routine, with its habits and techniques, weaves about us a soft cocoon, we sink into a lethargy blindly leading us to death, and the objective responsiveness to our own existence becomes abolished. Travel drags us out of this ambush, inconsiderately snatches us away from the comfort and torpor in which we are entombed. "Far from home and friends, separated from our language, snatched from our props and stays, deprived of our masks (we don't know what the bus fare is, and everything is like that)," we come unexpectedly and with a certain perspective upon life which but a short while ago had caught us in its toils. Our "inner décor" collapses, and we rise "to the surface

---

[16] Essay, "Collection Méditerranéennes," Algiers, 1937. The author has opposed a reissue of the five narratives which constitute this work, because he is not entirely satisfied with their form.

of ourselves," we have become detached. Thus we confront our veritable selves, are at the same time very close to and very far away from "the man that we were at home and who, at a distance, seems like a stranger." It is then that anguish looms.

After that self-confrontation, the traveller is not long in encountering the "density" of the world. The illusions of which he has just been stripped had given him support, surrounding him with a universe of familiar perceptions, gestures, words, and ideas; confronted, now, with an unmasked, mute, and impenetrable universe, the traveller feels lost in the confusion of an intensified consciousness, bared to the quick. The "discord which comes about between himself and things" gives an artlessness to his vision of the world, endowing the most ephemeral and humble of realities with the unique fact of existence, thus restoring to each living thing, each object, its miraculous worth. Now, the miracle, because it is in itself its own end and definition, repudiates the conscious mind that seeks to comprehend it. Excluded by the images he affronts, man henceforth embraces nothing but his solitude and exile.

"The divorce between man and his life," wrote Camus in *Le Mythe de Sisyphe* (p. 18), "between the actor and his setting, this is, strictly speaking, the sentiment of absurdity."

And yet . . . "Yet, in the train that was taking me from Vienna to Venice, I was expecting something . . . . A light was dawning. I know it now, I was ready for happiness."

We see that happiness resolving itself into the complicity of pure Mediterannean landscapes, experiencing its true form, recognizing its realm, defining its rhythm.

The four essays that comprise *Noces* are presented a little like that "gospel of divestiture" which Camus, after his illness, was to discover in Gide's *Les Nourritures Terrestres*.[17] To judge by the first pages, filled with a calm and passive euphoria that is simultaneously barbaric and refined, one is tempted to see in this work a new "Song of Songs of Immoralism," brimming over with sensual joy, a book which almost procures for the reader a physical contact with the gardens it celebrates.[18] But upon looking closer, the lyricism of the North African manifests a more vigorous effusion of animality, whereas the immoderate outpourings of his

[17] *Hommage à André Gide*, pp. 223-228, N.R.F., Paris, 1951. An interesting point is that Gide wrote *Les Nourritures* upon recovering from an illness and Camus the essays in *Noces* shortly before his illness. True, this does not explain the opposition of their "amoralisms" —one should rather find that explanation in the fact that a generation separates them—but it is certain that in the beginning this difference of experience could only strengthen the differences of dispositions.

[18] Göran Schildt, *Gide et l'homme*, p. 56, *Le Mercure de France*, 1949.

predecessor postulate but a cerebral backfiring. Not surprisingly, Camus himself detected this flaw: "Something . . . in this admirable exaltation smacks of conversion,"[19] which he found disconcerting. Moreover, a note at the bottom of page 59 unambiguously states what he thinks of "the sensual asceticism" of his elder: "May I be so foolish as to say I do not like the way Gide exalts the body? He wants to hold his desire in check to make it keener—which puts him in the company of those men who, in the *argot* of brothels are called "the involved ones," or "the cerebrals."

Noces à Tipasa: what a riot of color and perfume and tactile sensation! Here, at this rendezvous of stone, sea, and sun, the body achieves Dionysiac supremacy. "How many hours spent trampling underfoot the fragrant herbs, caressing the ruins, trying to accord my breathing with the tumultuous sighing of the world. Submerged among the wild odors and somnolent concerts of insects, I open my eyes and heart to the intolerable grandeur of that sky gorged with heat." (p. 16) On the level of absolute brute sensation, from which the conscious mind is alienated, he recovers his profound harmony with nature. And, entrenched in the cool shadows, having abandoned himself to "the happy

[19] *Le Figaro Littéraire*, February 24, 1951.

lassitude of my nuptials with the world," he listens to
the silent harmonies within himself and feels the pride
of living in all its plenitude. "I had performed my functions as a man, and to know joy throughout a long
day did not seem to me an exceptional feat, but the
awed accomplishment of a condition which, in some
circumstances, makes happiness a duty." (p. 28) Pagan
song of deliverance, this is a kind of virile paean to the
glory of sensual joys.

But now we have *Djémila*, with its vestiges of the
past, Djémila, a town of the dead. One of those places
"where the mind perishes so that a verity may be born
which is negation itself." In the eye of the wind that
impetuously harries it, the self is burnished, "worn
down to the soul," and progressively assimilated to the
arid landscape of ruins, as if at last summed up in "the
solitude of an antique column or of an olive tree out-
lined against the summer sky." Through his identification with the landscape, the wanderer experiences
that detachment from himself which the traveller of
L'Envers et l'Endroit had known in the depths of an
exiled consciousness. "Soon, scattered to the four corners
of the earth, forgetful and forgotten by myself, I am
in and of this wind, these columns and this arch, these
flagstones that feel hot and those pale mountains around

the deserted town." (p. 38) He *is* what he lives, he is "as if imprisoned for eternity—and everything is present to him." The past dissolves, the future is unthinkable, and the present is so intense that the flesh is borne to the farthest frontiers of its possessions, fiercely setting the individual against everything that would oblige him to renounce this newly recognized weight of life. "I do not like to believe that death opens upon another life. To me it is a door that shuts." (p. 41) The great lesson of *Djémila*, is "the conscious certitude of a death without hope." Exaltation and bitterness: between these two poles oscillates the tragic happiness of the man.

L'Eté à Alger takes up again this teaching ("Everything here breathes the horror of dying in a country that invites us to live"), and offers us a collective illustration. "This entire people, flung into its present existence, lives without myths, without consolation; it has invested all its wealth in this earth, and thereafter is left without defense against death." (p. 77)

Le Désert pictures the intolerable beauty of Tuscany —the unchanging aspects of its art, the changing aspects of its countryside—which dissimulates beneath a profusion of enchantments the same illuminating truth: that of the flesh overwhelmed with sensual delight, that of the consciousness emptied of hope. Here too the mind learns that it is nothing and that its sole reason for being is the perishable body, precisely because perishable. In "this desert magnificent to the heart" it is impossible to allow oneself to be beguiled by myths. Denied, excluded, or admitted, brought down to the measure of his destiny, man has a presentiment that "a certain continuity in despair can engender joy." (p. 110) That "divestiture" rejoins a greater wealth, and that certitude of death a higher passion for living.

One day, from a hilltop terrace, we witness with him "the great breathing of the world," and glimpse, with him, the possibility of "a higher happiness, where happiness seems futile" (p. 114), the happiness that unfolds in contemplation. "The world is beautiful, and beyond it there is no salvation." (p. 117) The traveller succumbs to the sweetness of that privileged moment: "I admire, I admire that bond which, in the world, unites mankind, that double reflection in which my heart can intervene and dictate its happiness to the precise bounds where the world can then complete or destroy it." (p. 122)

In this poetic luxuriance of ideas which, matured by age and selected and organized by reflection, will take form in his later works with well defined outlines, may already be seen the constants of the thought of Albert

Camus. First of all, there is his atheism,[20] which is not the negation of the divine but the impossibility of opening his heart to the revelation of any kind of absolute truth, a rejection which, on the one hand, determines his lucid adhesion to the only relative truths of earthly existence, and on the other hand, a kind of dynamic imperative which keeps him from sinking into despair and secretly hands him over to reasons of the heart which his mind does not know.

2. NIHILISM AND A PROVISIONAL ETHICS

When, in 1942, *L'Etranger* appeared, the book created a sensation and provoked the greatest variety of reactions. As a matter of fact, it was almost impenetrable or was badly understood, and it was necessary to become acquainted with *Le Mythe de Sisyphe* which appeared a few months later, in order to measure its real scope. In effect, this book of essays describes and comments upon the awareness of the absurd which comprises the climate of *L'Etranger*. Since the narrative aimed at inspiring the *sentiment* of the absurd, and the essay the *notion* of the absurd, it goes without saying

[20] Adopting a distinction that Gabriel Marcel had explained, Charles Moeller ("Albert Camus ou l'honnêteté désespérée," pp. 42 *et seq.*) concludes that Camus' atheism is more *a refusal of God* than the *impossibility of God*. Certainly his atheism makes him refuse any effort to find a transcendent truth.

that to explain the former we must benefit by the enlightenment furnished by the latter.

Le Mythe de Sisyphe (The Myth of Sisyphus)

The absurd, and suicide. "There is but one truly serious philosophical problem: it is suicide." Thus the book of essays begins. It is but a means for the author to give impetus to his thought. Suicide would not preoccupy him if it did not respond to the most pressing of questions: the meaning of life. And that response is resumed in the avowal that "It is not worth the trouble." The traditional explanations of suicide, sentimental or other, all imply the same profound cause, which is, that the individual, sustained until then by habit, suddenly discovers "even instinctively, the ridiculous character of habit, the absence of any profound reason for living, the senseless character of that daily agitation and the futility of suffering." (p. 18) This desperate illumination is what Camus calls "the sentiment of the absurd." It remains to judge if this sentiment or feeling finds its necessary conclusion in suicide. But before deciding this, the author gives himself over to an examination of the "absurd walls" within which is played out the drama of our human condition.

The absurd walls. The sentiment of the absurd, unexpected, unforeseeable, "in its light without radiance," can strike anyone anywhere at any moment. The very banality of daily life constitutes a medium particularly favorable to its emergence. "Get up, take tram, four hours at the office or factory, lunch, take tram, four hours of work, supper, sleep, and Monday, Tuesday, Wednesday, Thursday, Friday, Saturday, at the same rhythm this course is easily followed most of the time." (p. 27) Until the day when weariness causes a sudden awakening of the conscience. Why, of what use this mechanical existence, what rhyme or reason is there in it?

Another vision of the absurd. We enjoy making plans for the future, although "after all, it's a question of dying." But the time comes when the scales fall from our eyes and we see that beneath its mask Time is a sly enemy and not a faithful ally. We count on time's giving us its support, and implacably and ceaselessly it situates us on our course—"Thirty years old, already!"—weighing upon us, exhausting us.

Then, too, what can be said of the staggering shock we receive when we suddenly perceive "to what extent a stone is foreign and irreducible to us, with what intensity nature or a landscape can repudiate us"? (p. 28) And when we ourselves are astonished at seeing "the stranger who, at certain moments, comes to meet us in the looking-glass, the familiar and yet disquieting

brother that we find in our own photographs"? (p. 29)
And when, in the face of a beloved one, it happens that
we do not recognize anything in those eyes, that mouth,
that forehead that we have so loved? All these privileged moments brutally confront us with the absurd
and then leave us, self-denounced, in its pitiless light.

How may all this be explained? Simply by the unexpected contact with the reality of creatures and things.
For that reality usually eludes us. Our habits conceal
it, our affective life camouflages it. Stripped of these
disguises which our conscious mind endlessly compels
reality to assume, it looms up in its strict objectivity,
"foreign," inhuman, and repellent. It is here that we
find the absurd lying in wait for us.

But where, without denial, the absurd assails us, is
when we confront death. This, naturally, has nothing
to do with the experience of the thing. Nor, still more,
with the death of others. "The horror comes in reality
from the mathematical side of the event. . . . That ele-
mentary and definitive side of the adventure is the
entire content of the sentiment of the absurd. Beneath
the mortal illumination of this destiny, the futility of
it appears. No moral code, and no least effort are *a
priori* justifiable, considering the ruthless mathematics
controlling our condition." (p. 30)

To the inventory of the sentiments "which can comport something of the absurd" succeeds that of the efforts of the mind condemned to the same impediment: to the confusion of the sensibility is added the impotence of the intelligence.

In line with Montaigne, Pascal, Poincaré, the author demonstrates the infirmity of our understanding: the incapacity of distinguishing the true from the false, the impossibility of knowing oneself and the world, the vanity of scientific enterprise, in a word, the resistance of multiple and elusive reality to our unity and clarity.

The fact remains nonetheless that the clairvoyance acquired in the humiliation of our powers allows a more exact definition of the absurd. The absurd, we have let it to be understood, is everything that has no meaning. But the world appears thus to us only because it eludes our reasoning, and our own life shows up the same character only in the same divorcement. We are thus justified in concluding that the absurd depends upon neither the one nor the other of the elements present, but upon their confrontation. "The irrational, the human nostalgia, and the absurd that emerges from their confrontation, these are the three characters of the drama." (p. 45)

Absurd, the contradiction between our aspiration for the eternal and our subordination to duration; absurd, the opposition between our desire for unity and the irreducible duality of our nature; absurd, the discord between our passion for understanding, for exercising our reason, and the unintelligibility, the "unreasonable silence" of the world, between our feverish quest for happiness and the vanity of our action.

In his enumeration of absurd experiences, Camus has never ceased making it clear that only their consequences interested him. The moment has come to apply the findings.

Philosophical suicide. We cannot honestly consider it possible to solve a problem if we do not respect the admitted facts. We are therefore not authorized to elude one sole term of the question posed by the absurd. And this, be it recalled, is inscribed in a perpetual confrontation, "a struggle without respite." On the one hand, the irrational and incomprehensible; on the other hand, our impotence, from which naturally follows "the total absence of hope—which has nothing to do with despair—a continual refusal—which must not be confused with renouncement—and a conscious insatisfaction—which should not be assimilated to youthful unrest." (p. 50)

And yet a response has been given which destroys the equation to be solved. Camus has called it "philosophical suicide" because it repudiates lucid reason and, without that lucid reason, the absurd ceases to exist. Camus alludes here to some metaphysical themes of

Jaspers, Chestov, and Kierkegaard, whose experiments had been analyzed, along with others, in a preceding paragraph. (p. 39 *et seq.*) Now, that experiment was to conclude with a clever juggling of the problem. The religious faith which serves as axis to these philosophies introduces the notion of hope into the debate, thus suppressing one of the terms of the imposed confrontation. If our exile here on earth must be resolved and justified one day in the contemplation of the celestial realm, the irrational (in its essence) becomes rational (by its existence). The obstacle is circumvented; the experiment aborted.

The conscious mind upon awakening, began by recognizing its prison, then at once invoked hope to drive away that bad dream; after thus having dispelled the "walls" which enclosed it, the mind found an escape— but into the night of routine living, where it soon fell asleep again.

Now that we hold that to be conscious of the absurd and to remain so is to persist in recognizing our imprisonment and the impossibility of appealing the sentence of death to the supernatural or to some kind of hope, nothing prevents us any longer from returning to the problem of suicide which we have left pending.

Life has no meaning, therefore I kill myself. Logic is satisfied. Perhaps one can say as much of the demands of truth brought to light in a movement of clairvoyance? I kill myself, and I annihilate with me this conscience in which the vision of the absurd finds its support. I destroy the confrontation, I "skip" the problem, I vault over it. Hope denies the opacity of the world by substituting for it the transparency of divine reason; suicide denies our need for impossible transparency, comes to grief on that same opacity, and admits the absurd, that is to say, avoids it. We must live, if we wish to maintain what we believe to be true.

"To live is to make the absurd live. To make it live is, above all, to face it squarely. Unlike Eurydice, when we avert our gaze, the absurd dies. Thus, revolt is one of the few coherent philosophical positions." (pp. 76-77) For revolt, setting human reason and the inhumanity of the absurd face to face, inaugurates a perpetual struggle in which the mind, "eternally renewed, eternally on the alert," remains wide awake. That is what gives life all its value. "For a man without blinkers, there is no finer spectacle than that of the intelligence at grips with a reality that transcends him." (p. 78)

The revolt cannot expect any compensation for its lucid, lonely, and continued effort. It is a revolt without hope; it defends its truth, that perishable flame which leaped forth one day from the burning centre of the consciousness, and maintains it. And the heroic zeal of this revolt seeks for nothing except to prove human grandeur.

However, one must live. A man must consciously resume "the chain of daily gestures" but with a new disposition, a new virtue. This consciousness which, before the absurd experience, allowed itself to be sunk in a comfortable lethargy, will henceforth sustain its vigilance and exercise the freedom recognized in its definitive awakening. Since nothing of what can be thought or done has any meaning, my life is no longer inclined towards, one thought rather than another or to accomplish this thing rather than that. Without aim, without plan for the future, shut against all those hopes which would have compelled a constant choice, that is to say, a renouncement, a discipline of action, that is to say, self-restraint, the absurd man sees opening to him a total liberty, which the perspective of death increases and exalts still more. The "absurd" man, being solicited by nothing, is disposed to and available to everything. And death, upon which he stubbornly fixes his gaze, frees him without appeal, discharging him from all responsibility. The old freedom, that freedom which he believed he experienced when it was a matter of "thinking of the future, deciding upon an aim, having a preference," was only an illusion, threatened at every turn by death. "Absurd" freedom, placing existence in the perspective of death, diverts the attention of the individual from his aims, that have suddenly become paltry, and concentrates it upon the will to live.

Since God does not exist and since one must die, everything is allowed. But if everything is allowed, everything is indifferent. There can be no question of establishing a scale of values among the experiences that life proposes. "The important thing is not to live better but to live more." (p. 84) An ethic of quantity which rejoins and even supposes an ethic of quality. For it is not by accumulating the most varied aspects of the sentient world that we live most, but simply by being lucid, by "being aware of one's life, one's revolt, one's freedom as much as possible . . ." To taste fully the passing moment, to pause at each and to lose none, "To keep each successive moment before the mind unceasingly conscious, is the ideal of the absurd man." (p. 88)

Three types of man make of this ideal the ferment of their existence: the lover, the comedian, the adventurer. Their portrait is sketched in the second chapter, *"L'Homme Absurde,"* with the understanding that these extreme cases of the absurd man are not put forward as examples but as illustrations of a consistent attitude. As for the "most absurd of absurd men," the creative man, it was considered that he deserved to have a special study devoted to him, *"La création absurde"* ("Absurd Creation"), which we will deal with in a separate chapter.[21]

But the man in the first rank, the one who summarizes all and whose destiny gave birth to one of the most poignant myths of antiquity, is Sisyphus. The gods had condemned him to roll to the top of a mountain an enormous mass of stone which, when it had barely reached its destination, rolled back towards the depths from which he tirelessly raised it up again. "If this myth is tragic, it is because its hero is conscious. Where, in effect, would be his suffering if at each step he were sustained by the hope of succeeding? . . . Sisyphus, proletarian of the gods, impotent and rebellious, knows the whole extent of his miserable condition: that is what he thinks about as he makes his descent. The clairvoyance which constitutes his torment consummates at the same time his victory. There is no destiny but what can be surmounted by disdain." (pp. 165-166)

As may be seen, it was inevitable that Camus' essay on the absurd should be entitled *Le Mythe de Sisyphe*.

L'ETRANGER (THE STRANGER)

An authoritative critic, Marcel Girard, has stated that with this work Albert Camus has provided "the best

[21] See our Chapter III.

novel of his generation."[22] Upon rereading it, we cannot, in any case, refrain from applying to it the reflection made by Jean-Paul Sartre in regard to a novel of Faulkner: "With the recoil of time, good novels become as like as possible to natural phenomena; we forget that they have an author, we accept them as we accept stones or trees, because they are there, because they exist."[23]

L'Etranger belongs in reality to the category of narrative rather than to that of novel. The plot is simple. (Before all else, let us especially note that the action takes place in Algiers and its vicinity. We could even say, as will soon clearly appear, that it is inconceivable elsewhere.)

The hero-narrator is a humble employee, one of those creatures whose humdrum existence contains nothing worth noting. He is Mr. Anybody. Meursault, as he is called, has just learned that his mother has died in the Home for the Aged where he had finally been obliged to place her three years previously. The very day after the funeral, he strikes up an intimate friendship with a girl, Marie Cardona, a stenographer formerly employed in the office where he works, meeting her by chance

[22] Marcel Girard, *Guide Illustré de la Littérature française moderne*, 1918-1949. Paris, 1949.

[23] Jean-Paul Sartre, *Situations I*, p. 8. Paris, 1947.

at the bathing beach in the harbor. But this changes nothing in his way of life, no more than does his bereavement. On Sundays, Meursault is bored, and during the week he tries to put in some honest work and not to displease his employer. Of course, there's Marie, from time to time, Marie who has asked him if he loves her and to whom he has replied that the phrase meant nothing but that he felt he did not. Marie, who has asked him to marry her, and to whom he has replied that he would do it "whenever she liked." Marie, in short. There was also the offer his employer had made to create a job for him in Paris. But for Meursault it's all the same: to marry or have a simple affair, to live in Paris or to live in Algiers.

Then, one Sunday, a fellow lodger by the name of Raymond, to whom he had had occasion to render a service, invites him to spend the day, with Marie, at the home of a couple of friends in the suburbs. Everything would have been for the best if our men had not had a scuffle on the beach with some Arabs who had followed them that far, having a grudge to settle with Raymond. It is at Raymond that their blows are aimed, and he is the one who receives the blows and after having been somewhat repaired, it is he who decides to turn upon his aggressors. Meursault, who accompanies him, and to whom he has entrusted his revolver, finds himself alone at a given moment, "Come there without having thought about it," standing in front of the last Arab. What matter! In his mind, "the affair was finished." But the Arab pulled out his knife, "the sunlight glanced off the steel." Blinded by the sweat that had accumulated in his eyebrows and now suddenly runs down over his eyelids, Meursault controls himself no longer but pulls the trigger.... Then, he fires again, "four times on an inert body where the bullets sank in without leaving a visible trace."

Imprisonment, investigation, trial: the judicial machinery swings into action. The witnesses testify that the accused had not wanted to look at his dead mother, that he had smoked, slept, and drunk coffee during the funeral vigil, and that next day he had even gone to see a Fernandel movie! The indictment emphasizes that "when he buried his mother he was already a criminal at heart." Meursault is condemned to be guillotined.

The hope of a still possible appeal torments him for quite awhile. And then it is that the prison chaplain, whom he has refused to see many times, enters the death cell: after the temptation of hope, the temptation of salvation. Irritated by proposals that do not interest him, anxious not to lose what little time remains in hearing about God, who represents nothing to him, Meursault can no longer contain himself. He revolts, unleashes a storm of abuse; his consciousness pierces the darkness, revealing to him the sentiment of the absurd and the knowledge of his innocence; his past revives, disclosing to him that he has been happy—and still is, so close to annihilation . . .

Here we have the essential themes of *The Myth of Sisyphus* illustrated: the moral blindness of daily automatisms, the temptation of hope confronting death, and revolt. There remains one other theme: the rage to live. This theme is carried out poetically, in a style that is ample and colorful, on the last page of the narrative. "The Stranger," henceforth lucid, tastes with rapture the immediate moment; the man condemned to death, at last drawn from his lethargy, awakens to life and comes to terms with "the benign indifference of the world," that exterior world "which can always deliver us from everything," as the author of *La Peste* would later write.

What could quite possibly one day designate this little book of 150 pages as one of the classics of our century is not, we may be sure, the simple fable it relates, but rather, on the one hand, the sentiment of the absurd which emanates from it and, on the other hand, the art with which it proceeds, an art in which construction and technique of style perfectly adapted to its needs both play their part.

The sentiment of the absurd. The demonstration of *The Myth of Sisyphus* gives us the key to *The Stranger,* it is true. However, we must renounce seeing in the novel a romantic prefiguration of the essay. The novel explains nothing, proves nothing; it is not a novel with a thesis to expound. It does not show us a man, struck one day by the notion of the absurd and desperately seeking to escape from his "nausea," then, on the verge of suicide, operating that sudden recovery which mobilizes him in a conscious revolt, making him measure his t. edom and arousing his passion for earthly experience. No. Meursault does not know the awakening of consciousness until the end of his adventure, on the last page; but it is remarkable that up to then his life has obeyed, according to all appearance, the absurd orthodoxy. He therefore presents this singular case of a conscious mind lulled to sleep but linked with a behavior that supposes a wide-awake state.

With Meursault, the absurd is like a congenital infirmity, and this is what gives such weight of reality to his character. One might say that the absurd is in his blood. And he makes that absurd live, not by the vigilance of the mind, but in the abandonment of the flesh. By his intense physical presence, Meursault is indeed the brother of those young "barbarians" of the Mediterranean shores that were evoked by Camus in *Noces*.

Entirely given over to sensation, he lives only in the successive moments, and with the sensation that disappears, the moment vanishes before a memory of it can be organized and registered. Thus we have this man's incapacity of experiencing a feeling, for to experience a feeling presupposes continuity; he is without a past, but also without a future. The "It's all the same to me" that constantly returns to his lips is understandable. In order to express a judgment of value, it is necessary to base oneself on memory or have an imagination as to the future. In the flow of the present, all hierarchy is void of meaning.

Insensibility, indifference, absence of feelings, "inhumanity," this comprises more than is needed to elicit our avowal that Meursault has appeared to us as a "stranger." He is also a stranger to himself, since he cannot manage to give a meaning to his life, since "time . . . is for him nothing but a succession of distinct moments which no Cartesian God joins together and since he is traversed by no *élan vital,* and is transfigured by no memory."[24] And finally, he is a stranger to those

[24] Rachel Bespaloff, "Le Monde du Condamné à mort" in *Esprit,* January 1950, p. 2.

who approach him. Some, like Marie, will love him "because he's odd"; others will hate him, and to such a point that they will make him pay with his life for the horror he inspires in them.

It is not the man who has killed another man "on account of the sun" that society condemns, but indeed this kind of monster who refuses with unequaled firmness to enter into the game of their illusions, lies, and hypocrisies. Society wants a reassuring attitude from him and he does nothing but denounce, by his tranquil stubbornness in speaking the truth, the real and miserable aspect of man's fate.

In short, the murder he has committed is taken as being a pretext to destroy the truth that he embodies. That is what has made some people see in him "as it were, the negative proof of that Christ who came down to earth to be a man among men two thousand years ago."[25] For he is innocent, he does not assume the least guilt. In making a victim of him, society has merely recognized and proclaimed the scandal of human existence, to which he has witnessed forcefully throughout the trial, in his imperturbable identification of human existence with himself.

It is also hard not to discover the tragic background of this adventure. The theme of the sun, which blazes

[25] P. Néraud de Boisdeffre, *loc. cit.*, p. 306.

out in the essential pages of *Noces*, is here developed mysteriously, with the obsessive urgency of a leitmotif. Meursault will be only "the stranger," as a fictional character; he will not arrest our attention more than Voltaire's Ingénu or Candide. But his physical presence is affirmed, and physically it is subjected to an implacable sun. His blood is aroused, it would seem, only to take stock of this fatality which he feels he must endure. Through it, ineluctably, is accomplished his destiny as an individual, and this, in three phases: the funeral, the crime, the trial, each with its particular sun presiding. Roland Barthes, to whom we owe this very pertinent insight,[26] thus analyzes the tragic progression: "The funereal sun of the beginning is nothing more visibly than the condition of the sliminess of matter: the sweat of the faces, the softening of the asphalt along the torrid route of the funeral procession, here everything is an image of stickiness in the environment. Meursault is as glued to the sun as he is to the rites themselves, and the solar fire has as function to ensnare and shed light on the absurdity of the scene. On the beach, another figure of the sun: this one does not liquefy, it hardens, transforms matter into metal, the sea into a sword, the sand into steel, the gesture into

[26] *Club*, Bulletin du "Club du meilleur livre", April 1954, No. 12, p. 7.

murder; the sun is a weapon, a blade, a wedge, likely to wound, to mutilate, whereas the flesh of man is dull and flabby. And in the courtroom where Meursault is judged, we have finally a dry sun, a dusty sunlight, the rusty sunbeam of the hypogeum." And he concludes: "As in the *Oedipus at Colonna* or in Shakespeare's *Richard II*, the conduct of the hero is doubled by a carnal itinerary which attaches us to his magnificent and fragile existence. The novel is thus founded not only in philosophy but also in literature: ten years after its publication, something in this book continues to sing, continues to rend us; which is, indeed, the double power of all beauty."

The construction. The work is composed of two parts of equal importance. The first part makes us live beside Meursault a few of his days, and ends with the murder; the second makes us relive these same days, but obliquely, through the proceedings of the law court —depositions of witnesses, indictment by the Prosecuting Attorney—and *outside* Meursault. On the one hand, the insignificant life as it has been lived by the hero, a life without continuity, comprised of juxtaposed instants, "inorganic," one might almost say; on the other hand, the reconstitution of this life, gathered together and organized by the working of reason and the power of words. We see to what account the author expects to turn this confrontation: to bring to light the absurd in a display of the betrayals to which the mind yields in trying to apprehend the facts with the aid of concepts and language. This discord between the objective reality and the subjective image which pretends to reproduce it is calculated to penetrate us with the futility of human justice. How honestly support a verdict when its very object escapes all exact definition?

Meursault, in the prisoner's box, listens to what is being said about him, as though it concerned someone else; his absurdity emphasizes the absurdity of the miserable comedy in which his destiny is at stake and arouses a certain humor, which is perhaps the surest argument of the book.

But by what ingenuity does the novelist, using words like his Public Prosecutor, manage in the first part of his work to give us the illusion of being the direct witnesses of the reality which he evokes? This was a veritable challenge, which required the use of a special technique.

The technique of the style. Meursault, as we have said, lives only in detached moments, a succession of present instants independent of each other and cast back into oblivion once they have been consumed. This discontinuity of time is marked in the narrative by the discontinuity of the style.

Each sentence, like each instant, forms a whole, a small, homogeneous and enclosed universe, attached by nothing to what precedes, and drawing nothing in its wake. A thing is no sooner stated than swallowed up in silence; from one thing to the other, there is no logical articulation, no relation; in their juxtaposition, there is no trace whatsoever of some kind of spiritual ascendancy over reality. No consciousness interposes to organize this sensitive material, "translating" it and submitting it to the psychological selection which stocks the memory, unifies and orients it, projecting it into the future according to an affective dynamism. No. The narrator remains passive, his presence becomes transparent. Moreover, one might almost say that, above everything, he is preoccupied with remaining silent. Jean-Paul Sartre subtly noted this when he wrote ". . . his phrasing does not appertain to the world of speech, it has neither ramifications nor prolongations nor interior structure . . . it is measured out in the rhythms of a silent intuition."[27]

By imposing upon us an analytical vision of things, that is to say, by keeping them on a level lower than their significance, by preserving this same vision from the short-sightedness of habits and the deformations

[27] "Explication de *L'Etranger*," in *Situations I*, pp. 110-120. Gallimard, 1947.

of subjectivity, the discontinuity and the transparency of *The Stranger* puts us in contact with "pure" reality in the crude state, where lurks the absurd, to contaminate us. The awakening of the consciousness will inevitably follow, and thus the objective of the author will be achieved.

The conscientious conformity of technique with subject matter, so effective in application, is very like the prior achievement in certain of Hemingway's works, and leads to the supposition that Camus is responsible only for choosing to use it: he borrowed deliberately. The chapter on "absurd creation" in *The Myth of Sisyphus* strengthens this opinion.

It still happens that at certain moments, on certain pages, the warm and tender style of the poetic author of *Noces* furtively reappears, as if the dull and spasmodic flood of the absurdist aesthetic opened at times to allow the tide to rise from its depths, full and luminous.

But not only is there the style. In its composition also *L'Etranger* asserts its quality of a work minutely planned. Beneath its rambling, disconnected, dislocated appearance, this narrative shows a robust structural organization. Not one detail is left pending, but is utilized again at some point to weigh upon the hero's destiny. Such and such precise detail or incident, at first view futile and derisory, suddenly assumes, in the illumination of a new situation, a definitive and un-challengeable value.

On this score, this little book on the absurd can lay claim to the purest classicism.

B. DEVIATION AND DEVELOPMENT OF THE THOUGHT

1. THE TEMPTATION OF THE IMPOSSIBLE

Well within the solution brought to the problem of the absurd, we have the dark flame of a tragedy and the sinister parade of a drama. If it is kept in mind that the anecdote which is the basis of the play *Le Malentendu* ("Cross Purposes," in the English translation) is narrated in *L'Etranger* (pages 105-106),[28] and that a first version of *Caligula* was written in 1938,[29] it is not sur-

[28] "The author thus informs us that he stubbornly intends not only to create characters but human relations."—Emmanuel Mounier, in *Esprit*, January 1950, p. 28. Likewise, two lines in *La Peste*, page 68, recall the murder committed by Meursault.

[29] Charles Moeller is the only one, to our knowledge, who has felt in duty bound to accord a certain interest to this chronology. According to him, *Caligula*, written between 1937 and 1942, as Sartre has pointed out, would be seen to echo a crisis traversed by the author, rudely stricken by illness at that time. He who was born to sing the joy of life, and who did sing it, had had the revelation of the absurd in the humiliation of his flesh; and he transposed his personal drama into the impossible adventure of Caligula. According to this theory, the political romanticism of this dramatic work would be but window-

prising to find in these two plays the illustration of the conflicts which the thought of *Le Mythe de Sisyphe,* in a certain way, surpassed.[30] Let us rather admire how they were predestined in their time to embody in their symbolical significance the significance of contemporary events. Then, again, it appears that the author chose the themes of the absurd according to the category of expression which attracted him. Thus, the revolt of the humiliated, the vengeful, the bloody, finds its natural place in the theatre; the revolt of the oppressed, individual or collective, incapable of violence, finds its place in the form of the narrative. As Camus himself has said, in *Le Mythe de Sisyphe* (p. 155), it suffices that all his works be viewed together for them "to find their natural grouping."

---

dressing. Nevertheless, the fact remains that, by allowing a play written two or three years previously to be produced in 1944, Camus implicitly recognized that nothing in this work need be disavowed as not being in line with his thinking *at that time.* And all the same, we cannot do him the injury of thinking that he was unconscious of the political significance of the play at that period when the events of the day gave it a kind of double life. Moreover, the *Lettres à un Ami allemand* (the first two were known in 1944) are there to witness that *Caligula* well responded to the writer's preoccupations of the hour.

[30] The two plays, *Le Malentendu* and *Caligula* were published together by Gallimard in 1944. They were produced respectively in 1944 and 1945, the former at the Théâtre des Mathurins, starring Maria Casarès and Marcel Herrand, the latter at the Théâtre Hébertot, starring Margo Lion and Gérard Philipe.

LE MALENTENDU (CROSS PURPOSES)

In complicity with her mother, the sombre Martha, as a way of realizing her dream of sunshine and happiness, kills and robs and disposes of the bodies of travellers who stop off at their inn, situated somewhere in the rainy countryside of Bohemia. One day Martha's brother Jan comes back after twenty years of absence, happy to be able at last to bring the means of a richer life to those for whom he feels "responsible." Having maintained his incognito, considering that "it isn't enough, in such cases, to make oneself known," but that he must again "make himself be loved," he suffers the same fate as the transient guests that have preceded him.

When the "misunderstanding" is discovered, the mother drowns herself in the river into which they have cast the body of her son. Martha will also kill herself, but not before trying to destroy in Maria, Jan's wife who has come to ask for news of him, the illusion of any sentiment, the mirage of any possible significance in the human earthly adventure. In Act III, Scene 3, we have the following significant dialogue:

MARTHA: But I cannot die, leaving you with the idea that you are right, that love is not vain and this is an

MARIA: accident. For it's now that we are in the order
          of things. You must convince yourself of it.
MARIA: What order?
MARTHA: That in which no one is ever recognized.

Thus reechoes the theme of *L'Etranger:* in the universe without solace where we must live and breathe, we pass by each other without our own exile being able to enter into communication with the exile of others. That is what gives pathos to this play, in which the horrifying perspective of the crime seems to confirm itself from one moment to another in the contradictory rigidity of each of the characters who are now clear-seeing, now blind, according to whether the action concerns the individual or his relations to others.

Since sentiment cannot have any true basis, there remains nothing for the human being but to stifle the impulses of his heart and enter into the "blind peace" of the stone, or into the sleep of death. Martha gives no other advice to her sister-in-law. "You must choose between the stupid felicity of stones or the slimy bed where we will await you."

The voluntary achievement of indifference, or suicide —this is the alternative with which *Le Malentendu* confronts us. Maria, in an agonizing collapse will exclaim, "Oh, my God! I cannot live in this desert!" and will call upon the pity of heaven from the depths of her grief. A response will come from the lips of the old serving man, whose voice has not yet been heard, the old man towards whom she turns, imploringly. But his answer is "No." And that reply, which sets a final period to the tragedy, reveals to us, beyond the physical plane where we have seen the force of passion precipitate the action towards death, and beyond the moral plane where liberty in all things is allowed, and which ends in an impasse, a metaphysical plane where divine indifference has taken scenically the forms of absence, of silence, and of refusal.

The demonstration is made, all too well made, all too apparent.

Whereas Meursault weighed upon us with all his weight of flesh, obsessed us with the disquieting opacity of his character, and resembled us "like a brother," the protagonists of *Le Malentendu* do not always succeed in attaining this human dimension in which the abstract ideas of the tragedy could really come alive. For the greater part of the time they fall short of being themselves, cramped by the symbolical destiny the author has assigned to them, incorporated in it, instead of its being incarnated in them. The result is that, despite all the art of the playwright, who, in the strong and sober manner of the dialogue, provides us with scenes of rare plastic beauty, the work as a whole does not ring true.

Nevertheless, what is surprising is that this "dark play," fashioned on the pattern of the absurd, also shimmers secretly with that light which Camus has always carried within him and which he keeps alive, like a muted nostalgia of his past, and the most tenacious promise of the future. Of what does Martha dream? What desire impels her to accumulate her crimes? She yearns to escape this overwhelming landscape without horizons, this gray and enclosed universe in which she feels imprisoned, and to find the seashores spread out beneath the sun. In other words, to escape from the suffocation human beings know within "the absurd walls," and to taste happiness. It is clear that the young North African, when he calls up the vision of happiness, sees it always in sunlight. This theme, which the first essay of *Noces* and also the essay *L'Envers et l'Endroit* before it, expressed in the opposition between the "historical cities" and the walled cities, shut in upon themselves, privileged places, the seaside towns, open to the purest light, this theme which the adventure of *L'Etranger* weaves so powerfully, here attests its permanence at the centre of the artist's thought.

CALIGULA

Even if you are young and Caesar, you weep when you discover that "things are not as they should be." It needs but a sudden unsettling of the soul, for instance, the loss of the woman you love. Thus, one day, Caligula felt penetrated by "a quite simple, quite clear, and rather stupid truth . . . heavy to bear": human beings die, and they are not happy.

But because one is young, and especially because one retains absolute power, one may nourish the wild ambition to change the order of things, one may wish to "mingle the heavens and the sea, ugliness and beauty, make laughter spring from suffering."

SCIPIO: But it's a game without limits. It's the amusement of a madman.

CALIGULA: No, Scipio. It is the virtue of an emperor . . . Oh, my dear friends! I have at last comprehended the uses of power. It gives the impossible some chance. Today and for all time to come my liberty has no more frontiers.

The world has no meaning and no one seems to guess this truth? Well! We shall see to it that everyone has access to the truth of the world, "which is not to have any." "Rejoice! An emperor has at last been given you to teach you liberty." It is enough to push the absurd to its final consequences, that is to say, enough to be logical and remain unflinchingly so. Therefore, let us suppress all the traditional values which give existence an illusory significance.

Caligula begins by despoiling rich and poor alike, by turning the patricians to ridicule, then he kills the sons and the fathers of his friends, inflicts tortures, starves the people, degrades virtue, flouts conjugal love, raises lechery to the rank of civic duty, blasphemes, and ends up by strangling with his own hands a bothersome mistress. All this with the exhibitionism of a mountebank who seems to be applauding his own spirited performance. Caligula acts, and watches himself act, his "curious tragedy." How far will he go in his experiment with the impossible? His freedom has demanded everything of violence, to dress his revolt. But now he is crushed by a nameless solitude, a solitude "poisoned by presences" —the presences of his victims. Hate and conspiracy surround him, hemming him in ever closer, squeezing him as if in a vise. The impossible has not been attained. At the moment of paying, fear seizes him. But since nothing endures, and he is guilty! Stabbed by one of the conspirators, he shouts, as he expires, "I'm still living!" It is like a challenge to eternity.

Meursault, condemned to death, remained a victim. Caligula expiates his crimes as executioner. Certainly, for the one as for the other, all acts are of equal value and "to live is the opposite of to love." But Meursault kills by mischance, and is not enlightened by his revolt until the dawn of his punishment, whereas Caligula assassinates through reasoning, his point of departure being his freedom to revolt, through his absolute power.

What more closely relates *Le Malentendu* and *Caligula* is that we see in both the same temptation of the impossible, the same "superhumanistic" temptation. In both we have the "painful sentiment of impotence, the proud revolt against the injustice of such a humiliation, nostalgia for what man has been, might have been, could be, anguish caused by the idea of death; all this complex of passions constituting an intolerable psychosis for which must be found, if not a remedy, at least an alleviation."[31] Both Martha and Caligula have sought this remedy in the Nietzschean "will to power." Contempt for their condition has made them respond to life with arguments of force. What we cannot exceed, we destroy. But we are not long in becoming the prisoner of our crimes and of our sterility; defeat, then, authorizes but one attitude: the destruction of ourselves. And so we have the suicide of Martha, the "superior" suicide of Caligula. Between these two epilogues, as between the two experiments they conclude, there is but a difference of weight.

Let us not confine ourselves to the fictional aspects through whose intense romanticism may be discerned the political tragedy of our time. Today, still, "the

[31] Gabriel-Rey, *Humanisme et Surhumanisme*, p. 15. Paris, 1951.

misunderstanding" on the scale of peoples, nations, humanity entire (as Vercors bitterly has noted), demands that "men of good will cannot recognize each other."[32] As for the monstrous logic of Caligula-Hitler, we know only too well what it cost Europe and the world.

Nonetheless, this should not make us lose sight of the personal position of the author: a position that is both negative and expectant. In *Caligula,* he abandons the tyrant in obliging him to avow his error: "I did not follow the course I should have followed, and I ended up with nothing. My freedom is not the right one." In *Le Malentendu* he abandons the criminal mother by bringing her to foresee that "in a world where everything negates itself there are undeniable forces, and upon this earth where nothing is assured, we have our certitudes," which, in the event, is "the love of a mother for her son." And this double repudiation, without letting us presage the orientation of his future work, indicates a turning point, even so. Are we not assured that often "we recognize the path to follow by discovering the paths that lead away from it"?

If the temptation of the impossible is an enticement, if we must keep in mind "undeniable forces," then the liberty of the absurd man suffers a limitation; then

[32] Vercors, *Plus ou moins homme,* p. 329. Paris, 1950.

that revolt, the minute it recognizes and respects this limit, seeks to preserve something . . .

2. THE LESSON OF HISTORY

To our sorrow, Caligula made his reentrance upon the political scene, with the same destructive rage and with a nationalist mystique in addition. His ghost has been blamed; there is an effort to prevent his reincarnation. Let us explain.

The four *Lettres à un Ami allemand* simultaneously proclaim a breach with the past and a new examination of revolt and of the relations that should be established between absurd thought and action.[33]

A breach—which lets us suppose that the two friends were once in accord on certain points—is implied in the statement, "For a long time we were in agreement that this world has no superior reason for being, and that we felt frustrated . . ." (p. 75) A breach, since from identical concepts different and even opposing ethics have been inferred: "The thing is that you lightly agreed to despair and that I never agreed to it. You admitted

[33] These letters, which were to an imaginary friend, were "open letters," being published clandestinely during the German Occupation of France. The first was published in 1943 in the second issue of *Revue Libre;* the second at the beginning of 1944 in *Les Cahiers de la Libération;* the two others remained unpublished until all were collected in a volume issued by Gallimard in 1948.

enough injustice in our condition to bring yourself to add to it, while to me it appeared, on the contrary, that men should affirm justice in order to struggle against the eternal injustice, create happiness in order to protest against the universe of unhappiness. Because you pushed your despair to the point of rapture, because you unburdened yourself of it by setting it up as a principle, you agreed to destroy the works of man by struggling against him, in order to complete his essential misery. And I, refusing to admit this despair and this tortured world, all I wanted was for men to recover their solidarity, for the purpose of struggling against their outrageous destiny." (pp. 76-77)

Precisely, that destiny assumed for five years the aspect of the Nazi oppressor, and for five years the multiple front of the Resistance rose against him. How avoid drawing a parallel and remarking that the revolt against the absurd likewise springs from a suffering shared by all? How avoid having the feeling from then on that such revolt can justify itself only in the same human solidarity? Thus, the trials of the soul and body have revealed love.

The vision of death has, for its part, illumined another movement of the absurd thought. Caligula, slave of his reasoning, covers himself with blood in his effort to surpass the gods. Camus chooses justice, to remain "faithful to the earth." And he writes, "I continue to believe that this world has no superior meaning. But I know that something in it has meaning: it is man, because man is the sole being to insist upon having a meaning." (pp. 78-79)

It is no longer a question of pretending that everything is of equal value, that everything is allowed. The solution of *The Myth of Sisyphus* avers itself insufficient, confined as it is abstractly within the limits of individual conduct. From the moment revolt overflows this narrow framework, a new problem looms up, which is no longer that of suicide, but of murder. Reckoning from the fundamental absurdity, "Can or should one kill others?" Camus, as a French Resistant, replied in his own way. There remains to be seen whether his "taste for justice . . . as little reasoned as the most sudden of passions," can find in thought a reasonable foundation.

Solidarity and justice, love and respect for mankind, such are, on the frontiers of the absurd, the new points of view which will be stressed in the later works.

C. COMPREHENSION, WHICH GOES BEYOND THE ABSURD

1. THE TRUE HEALER

In 1945, Albert Camus takes his bearings. A little essay, *Remarque sur la révolte*,[34] marks the stage reached by his reflection and surveys the new aspect of his line of thought. "In the absurd experience, suffering is individual. From the first movement of revolt, it is the adventure of all . . . The malady which until then was suffered by one sole individual becomes collective plague."

Note, particularly, that word "plague" *(peste)*. Already, Caligula, having examined himself, had proclaimed the coming of the pestilence: ". . . in short, it is I who take the place of the plague." (p. 109) The word will be the title of the next narrative, and it is to be presumed that we should regard it as an extension of the essay.

LA PESTE (THE PLAGUE)[35]

La Peste was immediately hailed as an event. Only a few days passed after its publication in June, 1947,

[34] Published in the symposium, *Existence,* Gallimard, 1945.
[35] Published by Gallimard, 1947. Its publication in America as *The Plague,* had to wait until 1957.

before the jury of the Prix des Critiques asked the honor of awarding it their annual prize. The stir it created was tremendous. Translated into several foreign languages, it accomplished in six months the race towards world recognition which it had taken Malraux's *La Condition Humaine* fifteen years to accomplish (as the critic, Pierre Néraud de Boisdeffre put it).

And yet, in this wilfully drab narrative, ashen-hued, in this fresco as uncluttered as a diagram, nothing is conceded to imagination or sentiment, and everything is offered to the intellect. The assets usual to success are completely lacking; the indications of its worth are without adornment. To what may this paradoxical success be attributed? In fact, we believe that this work of simple realism presents, on different levels, a symbolical transparency, where each reader has been able to find something to satisfy his preoccupation of the moment, whether metaphysical, ethical, or historical.

The book is presented as being the diary of a witness who, in the final pages, is revealed to be one of the heroes of the adventure, Dr. Rieux.

It is a diary without circumlocutions, at the same time sober and detailed, measured and objective.

a) The Story.

The town of Oran, in no way more predestined than

any other to experience extraordinary events, and like-wise no better prepared than any other to endure them, is overwhelmed, in the year 194. . . , by the plague. The narrator sets out, in a simple narration, virile in tone, to describe simultaneously the progress of the epidemic, the behavior of the inhabitants, and the struggle against the pestilence undertaken by some of them.

The epidemic. This shows itself at first in curious symptoms: rats in ever growing number come to die in the streets of the town. Then, cases of fever, very troublesome, break out. After a slight retreat, the epidemic suddenly makes a new spurt. Confronted with the number of casualties, the Government stops shilly-shallying, proclaims the presence of the plague, and puts the town in quarantine: the gates of the city are shut and guarded by sentinels.

The plague insinuates itself, working methodically, without haste. Towards the end of the month of June, with the first wind that rises, its virulence is intensified. The statistics show seven hundred deaths a week. A second lot of serum received from Paris proves to be even less efficacious than the first lot. The statistics indicate a continuous rise in the death rate, while the disease takes a new form, becoming pulmonary. In the middle of August, at the time of greatest heat and wind, the disease reaches its culminating point. At the same time, it is seen to be moving from the outskirts of the town, where it seemed to be confined, towards the centre. Then come the rains of September and October: people wait expectantly for a change. But there is no change. The serum "manufactured with cultures of the very microbe infesting the town" is tried without immediate result. November comes: the daily hecatomb still reaches the same figure. Nonetheless, it seems that the epidemic has reached its peak. Succeeding its lightning-swift rise, there is a levelling off which, by some, is considered to be a reassuring sign. Nevertheless, with the cold days of December, upon which everyone had counted to stop the progress of the epidemic, it continues imperturbably to accumulate its assassinations with the same rhythm, the same regularity. "Yes, efforts must be renewed . . ."

One day, a case of pulmonary fever is checked just when all seemed lost. That first victory is to be shortly followed by others, Almost at the same time, the rats reappear, but alive, this time. The statistics finally indicate the recession of the epidemic. During the month of January, the serum, time after time, proves efficient beyond expectation. The plague is put to rout. After a few fits and starts, as of a wounded animal, it returns to "the unknown lair from which it had emerged, in silence."

The town of Oran reopens its gates and once more yields itself to carefree sleep.

The inhabitants. Their feelings could be inscribed on the same graph in two lines, one of which would interpret the progress of fear, the other the evolution of the emotive life separated from loved objects and dispossessed of affections. The former line would maintain itself for a certain time stationary, then would rise imperceptibly to the level of fright, then almost vertically to the acme of panic; it would then slowly zigzag down, stabilizing itself in a zone of dejection, and prudently would return, despite some oscillations of impatience, towards the zero of indifference and of blind tranquility. The latter line—of the emotive life—would shoot up almost in a vertical line to a sharp peak of heartbreak—separation, exile—would pass to the highest point of suffering, of the disembodiment of memory, then, sentiment having become emptied of all personal content, would adjust itself to the long waiting for the plague to withdraw; a contained, circumspect hope coinciding with the first victories over the disease, would then be led to an intermediary stage, from which it would plunge, after a few contradictory movements of excitation and depression, into the euphoria of reunions with loved ones, and of a resumed routine.

As for the reactions of the inhabitants, they are those

of any human community disturbed in its habits. These people who formerly gave themselves up to an existence devoid of suspicion, to the servile slumber of the absurd, will endure the absurdity of the plague with the same passivity. Most of them will elude it by stupefying themselves in cafés and cinemas. Some will seek a surer refuge in religion, with all the more application for having neglected it so long. Others, finally, the "sharp ones," will take advantage of the general disorder to go in for shady deals, and they will establish a kind of black market.

The fighters. Against this background of collective misery and egoistic preoccupations, some individuals in revolt against the plague are sharply silhouetted. These are the Rieux, the Tarrous, Ramberts, Grands, and Paneloux, who will organize the medical resistance against the epidemic and who, every day, will expose themselves to the contagion of each other's determination to make the cause of man triumph. Thanks to them, hospital units are set up, isolation camps are created, the burial of the dead is organized. The fighters are present on all fronts.

Although they have plunged unreservedly into this active work, they are not swamped by it. The harassing task which insensibly exhausts them, will never abolish in them the prerogatives of the mind. . . . On the contrary, in this daily contest with suffering and death, they commune with themselves, their thought takes precise form, with every nuance and illumination. During certain moments they steal from the tragic reality, the better to dominate it by reflection, discussion, the give and take of friendships; we are given a glimpse of the depth of their motives, and this obliges us to read beyond the fictional narrative.

b) Beyond the story.

The epigraph, which quotes Daniel Defoe, invites us to surpass the realism of the work—a symbolical realism—and to penetrate its veritable reality: "It is as reasonable to represent one kind of imprisonment by another, as it is to represent anything that really exists by that which exists not."

At the moment when the book appeared, minds barely delivered from the nightmare of the dark years of the war quite naturally were inclined to recognize the plague as being the German Occupation and the struggle against the epidemic as the very action of the Resistance. We must say that these transpositions offered no difficulty at all and that, in addition, enough was recalled of the author's militant attitude to make one feel authorized to make such transpositions.

But it would be narrowing the significance of the

work not to receive it except under color of an allegory inspired by circumstances. It would be to forget the reasoning of Camus, ever advancing since *Le Mythe de Sisyphe* and constantly being shaped by experience.

The *Lettres à un Ami allemand* have already given glimpses of the sense in which history had engaged the forward movement of Camus' thought. To discover that one is implicated in an adventure shared by others and that the same heartbreak establishes a complicity which it is impossible to evade—when one is called Sisyphus and carries within oneself the experience of all the Sisyphuses on earth—is to discover by analogy that one no more acts for oneself alone in the lucid revolt against the irrationality of the world than in the armed resistance to the oppression of the invader. In the individual, as in the general and organized revolt, the solidarity of human beings is revealed, and in return that solidarity brings its veritable justification to revolt.

Thus, the plague symbolizes at times this existence immured by the absurd, where we flounder about, and at other times, the evil witnessed by the suffering of the world and the sufferings of the innocent; at still other times, those baneful powers which work in us and which threaten, if we do not take care, to add still more to the misery of our condition. *La Peste,* rather than being an exalting of the Resistance, thus appears, in a roundabout manner, the manner of fiction, as a definition of a humanism faithful to human dignity and, in its widest bounds, despite its lack of the transcendental, a humanism open to a sacred interpretation.

It remains to be asked to what extent this work is, from the aesthetic point of view, a fable, and to what extent a realistic novel.

Certainly, its multivalent symbolism and the complexity of the decoding to which it lends itself, situates *La Peste* beyond the realm peculiar to allegory, the intentions of which are always clear and precise, allowing a simple tracing off, line by line. Furthermore, the content of each symbol does not coincide in all respects with the reality which informs it and the expression of the reality does not always attain the level of symbolism. Admitting for a moment that the plague represents the German Occupation, let us indulge in the game of equivalences: we will manage to establish a certain number of them, but we have to concede that historical reality is not exhausted by the narrative and that the narrative develops more than one theme without reference to historical reality. Thus, we search vainly, in this "anti-terrorism manifesto," for the symbol corresponding to the worst undertaking of terror and humiliation that men of our time have invented against their fellow men: the concentration camp. In other respects we may easily find in this narrative thousands of details, even episodes, which echo no historical event but which the logic of realism renders indispensable.

For this is the relation of an event—no doubt imaginary, but not unreal—that is to say, it is an objective relation of events situated in time ("in 194...") and space ("the town of Oran"). These events and the individuals involved in them, are presented to us by the narrator according to all the laws of probability. He may never have experienced any plague, but he has informed himself on the subject. Historically, to begin with: as witness this or that meditation of Dr. Rieux, this or that bookish recollection referred to in passing. Then, medically.

But never are the epidemic and its ravages evoked for their own sake. They constitute a framework of facts which subtend the expression of human suffering, the expression of revolt inspired by such suffering. And the writer assumes the existence of that revolt, not only through the attitude of his heroes but equally in the transfiguration he imposes upon reality. As was to be later specified in *L'Homme Révolté*, "Real literary creation . . . employs reality and only reality with all its warmth and its blood, its passion and outcries. It merely adds something that transfigures reality." (p. 333) That "something" here, is a summing up of the artist's protest against unjust conditions. That something, added to reality in Camus' work, causes the great wind of pity and sympathy which blows through it, prolonging and multiplying it beyond the anecdote in a cross-fire of symbols. We have only to imagine for a moment what Jean-Paul Sartre, for example, might have drawn from such a subject, what scenes of horror and violence, what trifling details his clinical eye would have brought to our notice, to form an exact opinion of the rebellious, slightly unfocused, stylized view that Camus gives of the world in *La Peste*, always ready to "satisfy the need for freedom and dignity in the heart of every man." "A cryptic realism," Rachel Bespaloff calls this realism which, while recreating reality, maintains the prerogatives of a rebellious consciousness and dispels the opacity of things, allowing the underlying thought to appear.

The protagonists. More than anything, the characters themselves represent a reply to the problem of evil. It is through them that the author pursues his search for an order of values in humanity's blind-alley existence. The characters have often been criticized for their lack of real solidity. One critic has even claimed not to see anything in them but a makeshift in the Camus order of aesthetics, and has asserted that obviously, had Camus been able to do so, he would have contented himself with a bare stage from which only voices would be heard, thus conveying his thought to us in all its conceptual purity. No doubt the prestige of this thought has hypnotized most critics, and the rather colorless sobriety of the tangible exhibits has been unable to counter what was, by and large, a biased reading. Nonetheless, it must be admitted that the physical descriptions of the characters often smack of the passport or the identity card, rather than of authentic fictional creations. Are we otherwise instructed as to their personality, their type, the characteristics that make each individual a unique and irreplaceable human being? Not very much.[36] Hence, when they confront each other in dialogue, we are always witnessing a confrontation, never a conflict of personalities.

If their creator withheld from them the keen breath of a passionately imaginative life, it is because he did not propose to launch them into the free exercise of their lives, allowing them to accomplish their destinies in their own way by the simple operation of their feelings. The rôle he assigned them is better defined and consequently more restricted, more linear. In effect, the life in which they are all equally caught up has plunged them suddenly into a night of misfortune, in-

[36] Grand, the most effaced of all the characters, must be excepted. Paradoxically he is the only one to possess real solidity; we shall explain this later on.

85

justice, and suffering, and in this crisis the demand that is made is not upon the entire individual but upon that part of him which concerns his dignity. Each one is expected to reply to the question that is put to all, at the same instant and in the same terms. And each one is a man confronting the condition of mankind, not an individual contending with his personal problems.

That is why, though their faces and souls remain in shadow, they compensate by demonstrating so strong a moral personality. The plague, far from infecting them, strengthens them; it is the test which reveals instead of dissolving, which concentrates instead of disconcerting; it is the fortuitous tragedy between the limits of which is expressed a drama much more vast, and which calls upon a man to specify the relations between his thought and his behavior.

Without being any one of his characters, even in opposition, Camus is no less found to be represented by all of them.[37] But each one of Camus' characters, diverse as they are, illustrates an aspect of his thought, and with all the more truth since that thought seeks to outdo itself in contradictory hesitations. But finally, given the right perspective, the thought appears, like a design in mosaics, revealing and reassembling its outlines.

[37] A confirmation of this may be found in Camus' remark on Sade: "A character is never the author who created him; but an author may quite likely be all his characters at once."

The thought. It is not without reason that the book opens with a description of the town and of the life that the inhabitants lead there, or that the author hastens to emphasize the banality of the setting—"to sum up, a neutral kind of place"—and the habits contracted there, which are like a natural secretion. The theme of automatism which daily weaves lives together was suggestively illustrated in the pages of *L'Etranger;* here it forms a backdrop sufficiently featureless for us to lose sight of the fact that these are citizens of Oran, sufficiently impersonal for us to discover here the very replica of our slumbering consciousness.

A stranger in town, "the stranger" being a certain Tarrou, about whom "no one could say where he came from or why he was there," records in his notebooks, with a visible penchant for the insignificant detail, his observations, reflections, and considerations as to people and things. In certain ways he rather resembles Meursault. He has the same taste for sensation, the same liking for the display of naked flesh on beaches and at watering resorts, the same mania for collecting trifles— Meursault keeps a scrapbook in which he pastes amusing pictures cut out of his newspaper, while Tarrou takes pleasure in collecting grotesque scenes, conversations devoid of interest, comic situations which he has caught in the net of his absurdist perception while strolling about the town. Identical behavior of the two characters, linked with different personalities. In contrast with his predecessor, Tarrou maintains himself in a condition of absolute lucidity. His voluntary exile and his unwonted diligence as chronicler appear in some kind of way as auxiliaries of this viligance. No doubt, Tarrou has read and pondered *Le Mythe de Sisyphe*. Nevertheless he does not seem to be at all set in his conclusions. We are intrigued when he says, "The only thing that interests me is to find inner peace." (p. 39) And when we hear him calmly affirm that he has no more to learn from life, we try to imagine the tormented past to which he could be referring. Yes, Tarrou has a story to tell, and one night, in an hour of friendship, he will tell it to Dr. Rieux.

It had all started that day when he was barely seventeen and had heard his father, a Prosecuting Attorney, demand in the name of society the execution of a convicted criminal. He was overwhelmed with an actual nausea, but held out against it for almost a year. Then, not able to stand it longer, he left home, resolved to defeat that society which was based on capital punishment. He joined a political party whose actions seemed to promise the establishing of a new order based on honor and respect for mankind, and threw himself body and soul into the struggle. Alas, in the new order as well as in the old, death sentences could not be avoided; he discovered that one is fatally led to assassination. One day he witnessed an execution and experienced the same vertiginous feeling that had overwhelmed him as a boy. This made him vacillate. The horror of the spectacle still haunted him. "Do you know that at such a short range the shooting squad aim at the region of the heart, and that with their big bullets they make a hole you could put your fist into?" (p. 275) Terrible but necessary sacrifices on the altar of an ideal! Thus Tarrou discovers that he has become an accomplice of evil in his effort to reduce it to impotence, and that no reason is admissible which, in any way, seeks to legalize murder. He withdraws from the combat. "From now on," he reflects, "I leave it to others to make history." (p. 278) He does not blame the others, he does not consider himself in a position to judge them, and he even continues to like them. Simply, he notes that it has become intolerable to be with them and to continue to be a plague-stricken person; that is to say, intolerable to have a heart contaminated by evil, a heart that finds nothing better than to consent to it or to become its agent. Henceforth, the only way to "comfort mankind and, if not to save them, at least to do them the least possible harm and even sometimes a little good," is to force oneself to attain to an inner purity by a constant and exhausting struggle against the microbe that one carries within oneself;[38] at the very least, "to watch oneself unceasingly so as not to be brought, in a moment of distraction, to breathe in someone's face and clap the infection onto him." (p. 277) But the fact remains that one always risks, despite the most scrupulous attention, ranging oneself on the side of the pestilence rather than on the side of the victims. Tarrou is not unaware of this. If it is permitted him to refrain from ever being a "reasonable murderer," he dares not depart from the modesty which allows him only to try to be "an innocent murderer." Executioners or victims; victims—executioners. "Naturally, there has to be a third category," and Tarrou cannot refrain from evoking this category, while measuring the distance which separates him from it: the category of the "true healers," of those who are content not only to attend the sick because such is their profession, but who, having vanquished the plague in the sick bodies, have let themselves be penetrated by love and uplifted

[38] Charles Moeller has in this connection noted the new preoccupation that Tarrou introduces into the universe of Camus: "With him, the theme of moral evil, the evil that men inflict upon each other, reaches its greatest depth." (*Op. cit.*, pp. 58-59.) And he recalls to mind (notes 8 and 12) the words of Scipio as to Caligula's scruples before his conversion to the absurd: "He often repeated that to cause suffering was the only way of fooling oneself." This comparison of ideas reveals the superior unity in which the thought of the writer shapes up from one work to another, as we have noted elsewhere.

by revolt, at contact with human misery. Their love of creation is such that their personal happiness is sought outside themselves, in a possible happiness for all the humiliated; their sentiment of revolt in face of creation is such that their professional action is sublimated in a hopeless struggle against death. Tarrou hastens to add that "one doesn't run across many of them," and that "it must be difficult." In concluding his story, he makes a final confession, which singularly clarifies the first. "Can one be a saint without God? That's the only concrete problem I know of today." (p. 279) Upon the experimental solution of this problem depends, in effect, the "inner peace" to which he aspires.

It is on the road which, beyond murderous innocence, leads to saintliness without God that the plague has caught Tarrou. We realize that it has taught him nothing, not even—especially not even—his solidarity with those who have chosen to combat it. For him, the epidemic represents a particular instance of the diffused and immanent pestilence, whose ethical and metaphysical modes of infection he has for a long time recognized.[39] Up to a certain point, one might perhaps even

[39] A question presents itself: does the author consider this evil as inherent in the nature of things, like an ineluctable fatality? Or, on the contrary, does he hold it as the penalty for an accidental weakness, a disorder characteristic of our time, a "psychosis" of the twentieth century? R.-M. Albérès makes the remark that "Camus still wavers

say the plague has come to confirm him in his inner convictions, and has allowed him to draw a little nearer the ideal which preyed upon his mind. We know that Tarrou helps Dr. Rieux to the very best of his powers. The plague lays him low at the very moment when victory appears to be, if not achieved, at least near. Rieux, who attended the dying Tarrou, does not know whether his friend found peace. There only remains in his heart the painful intuition that "for himself, there would never more be any possible peace."

To Dr. Rieux is entrusted not only the role of narrator but the mission of representing the type of "true healer". A narrator he is, because, having collected the most complete information on the history of this epidemic,

---

between these two positions," but that "in some of his writings he inclines towards the optimistic response, towards the idea that Evil is not totally congenital and that it can be historically surmounted." (*Les Hommes Traqués,* Paris, 1953.) He then cites this sentence in *La Peste* (p. 150): "The evil that is in the world almost always derives from ignorance, and good intentions, if unenlightened, can do as much harm as malevolence." Let us in our turn quote from the same page, a few lines farther down: ". . . the most incorrigible vice being that of ignorance which presumes to know everything and which therefore claims the right to kill." Without possible doubt, Camus is aiming here at the evil born of History, that evil of ideologies against which *L'Homme Révolté* will take such vehement stand. Already in 1948 Camus declared, in the course of an interview: "My personal position, as much as it can be defended, is to estimate that if men are not innocent, they are guilty only of ignorance. This idea should be developed." (*Actuelles,* p. 225)

he has felt it his duty to bear witness for the victims and to "tell quite simply what we learn in the time of pestilence, that there are more things to admire in men than to despise." (p. 336) A true healer he will be, not after having, like Tarrou, asked himself how to become one, but starting out with loving, in all humility, to do his duty, correctly and honestly. He, too, has his story. It is brief: "When I first entered this profession, I did it almost absent-mindedly, because I needed it, because it was a situation like any other, and one of those situations to which young men aspire. Perhaps also because it was particularly difficult for the son of a workingman such as I was. And then, I had to see someone die." (pp. 146-147) That was when something broke in him: his revolt, which raged against the very order of a world ruled by death. Death! That, certainly, was the worst of scandals! Bernard Rieux can no more believe in God than can Tarrou. For if man does not live in perfect innocence (what to say of his crimes, his wars, his injustices?) there are at least the children—and they die! But you cannot change the order of the world, and God does not exist. Faced with the seemingly hopeless situation, one feels the need to be more self-effacing.

The movement of revolt that springs from the vision of human suffering, while bringing to light the commonality of the condition which links him to his fellow men, renders the physician vulnerable to sympathy and shows him the meaning of the action to which he must dedicate himself: the struggle against evil. To attend the wound, the fracture, the organ attacked by the malady, the bubo and the dry cough, with the unique concern of rescuing sick bodies from suffering as rapidly as possible. To defend mankind against death, without losing sight of the fact that all victory is but temporary, and that sooner or later death will triumph. To *attend*, but not to *save*. Rieux clearly stipulates it to Father Paneloux: "Salvation is too big a word for me. I don't go that far. It's man's health that interests me, his health comes first." (p. 241) Thus, without circumlocutions, he affirms his determination for earthly happiness in the midst of a universe closed to the idea of any kind of salvation.[40] Having established "such a clear demarcation between the idea of happiness and the idea of salvation," as André Rousseaux has emphasized,[41] the novelist maintains his thought quite unequivocally.

[40] In January, 1945, Camus expressed himself in an editorial in *Combat* in the same terms, regarding an article by François Mauriac: " . . . We refuse to despair of mankind. Without having the unreasonable ambition to save men, we still want to serve them." (*Actuelles*, p. 74).

[41] "Albert Camus et la philosophie du bonheur," in *Littérature du XXe siècle*, Paris, 1949.

Moreover, it is by the logic of the same intellectual honesty that his mouthpiece declares himself to have no least taste for heroism and saintliness. This physician who is daily called upon to perform tasks without grandeur has remained in the very midst of the plague. True, he has had to extend his activity, has sometimes increased it to the verge of exhaustion; but within him nothing has changed, he has extended himself faithfully with an abstention that secures him against all false self-glorification and keeps him within the bounds of his ideal: *to be a man.*

The narrator does not fail to proclaim this priority of happiness in the very heart of his chronicle. "Let us give the truth its due," he specifies, "and heroism the secondary place it should have, immediately after, never before, the noble claim of happiness." (p. 157) It is therefore not astonishing to hear him approve the conduct of Rambert, the journalist, who, far from throwing in his lot with those struggling against the epidemic, does all he can to escape, spurred by his love for his mistress who has remained in Paris. Then we remember that Rieux has allowed his own wife, who has been ill for a year, to go away to a mountain resort, where she dies shortly afterwards. He loved her dearly. Why did he not go away, rejoin her? He could have surrounded

her with care, could have retarded her death or perhaps, who knows, could have cured her. Why, precisely,
should he have turned his back upon that happiness for
which the appetite of others seems to him so warranted?
We would not dare to reply since he has abstained from
doing so. "Nothing in the world is worth turning one's
back on what we love. And yet, I turn away, I, too,
without being able to figure out why." (p. 230) All the
same, in this blind and as if necessary choice of the
finest and most difficult action, something is revealed
to us of the force of an imperative transcending every
kind of moral reflection. A creative force. His conscience
torn, Rambert in his turn will not be long in feeling subjugated by it and irresistibly constrained to renounce
his egoistic resolve: "I've always felt I was a stranger
in this town and that I'd no concern with you. But now
that I've seen what I've seen, I know that I belong here,
whether I want to or not. This affair concerns all of us."
(p. 230) In vain was he told that "there's no shame in
preferring happiness," that if he wanted to share the
misfortunes of mankind, "there would never be time
for happiness." Nothing could shake his resolve. He had
chosen, he would stay, he would fight. And the conviction which dominates him in all its grandeur of shining
truth, though not supported by any value, founds and
inaugurates a new one: *There can be cause for shame*

in being happy all alone.[42] No sensitive heart can keep
from responding to human suffering with sympathy. A
fortiori, a heart in revolt against the absurdity of man's
fate.

Sympathy. A noble yet restrained sympathy blows
like a fresh breeze through the entire body of Camus'
work. You expect at any moment to have it break forth
in an effusion of warmth, but the author's sense of the
proprieties permits him only to use accents of sober
virility, as if he sought to avoid all prodigality.

To be moved to pity for a plague victim does not ever
signify, with Camus, a weakening, but rather the exchange of one's own exile with that of one's companion
in misery. How far we are, in *La Peste,* from the in-
communicable solitudes of *L'Etranger!* Here the barriers
are thrown down, the roads converge towards some high
destination. Faced with its condition, the human community tends to recreate itself from one individual to
another, within the bounds of a secret fraternity. Even
these "awakened sleepers" who constitute the majority
of the Oran inhabitants have in the long run come to
understand that "the plague concerns everybody."

[42] The youthful sensitivity which vibrates in the first essay of *Noces*
is content with a justification otherwise cramped: "There is no shame
in being happy." (p. 23) Which allows us once more to remark upon
how the theme of happiness, fundamental with Camus, is enlarged in
La Peste.

The human material of *L'Etranger*, buried beneath the greyish lava of insignificance, formed around the central character, rigid and colorless, a blur from which he emerged only to emphasize its disgusting platitude. In *La Peste*, the grey tints of the painting of absurdity are relieved by the pathetic highlights of flesh and blood; the outlines become clearer, the forms more vulnerable; the "pantomime devoid of meaning" of the human marionettes writhes occasionally in cruel and ridiculous convulsions but at times attains a deeply moving dignity. Pity spontaneously responds to suffering, and in some circumstances with such impulsive totality that the individual ceases to have a life of his own. For example, that page which Robert de Luppé has called "one of the culminating pages of the narrative, the blood-red rose-window of a cathedral," shows us Dr. Rieux *physically* sharing, rather than witnessing, the death agony of Judge Otho's child, anxious, as if by some occult transmission of vital force, to "sustain by his still intact strength" the suffering infant, seeking in a tension of his whole being to assume the burden of the innocent's torment.

Usually less exalted, the sympathy of the "true healer" reveals itself no less actively. The painful situations created by the event do not monopolize it. All suffering finds it responsive, even moral suffering, even sentimental, even obscure. The suffering of a Joseph Grand, for example.

This character resembles Meursault on more than one point. Like Meursault, he is a humble employee, in his existence as in his person; he presents "all the earmarks of insignificance." Even to the mysterious literary work that occupies his leisure time, he is identifiable with the "absurd" hero. His particular phrase, that phrase rewritten again and again, that first phrase of a novel that will never advance further, defines his limitations. The difficulty he has in finding the *mot juste* has always kept him from writing the letter of complaint which should set forth his legitimate rights to a promotion and explains why at his age he is still kept in a subordinate position, poorly paid. Although ambition has never spurred him on, nonetheless he had caressed the hope of a future that would amply assure him his material life while giving him the possibility of "indulging without remorse in his favorite occupations." Joseph Grand has, you see, an ideal.

But what finally differentiates him from "the stranger" and renders him so close to us is the quality of his sensitive and virtuous heart. "He did not blush to admit that he loved his nephews and his sister, his only surviving relatives whom he visited in France every other year. He admitted that the memory of his parents, who had died when he was still young, caused him grief. He did not hesitate to admit that he loved above everything a certain church bell in his neighborhood which softly pealed towards five o'clock in the afternoon." (p. 59)

One day this normally shy person, encouraged by the understanding friendship of Rieux, discloses his secret wound. Grand recounts his story, with a reserve that renders it very poignant. While still quite young, he had married a poor girl of his neighborhood. Monopolized by his office work, which held out hopes at the time, he had insensibly allowed the fire of his love to die down. "A man who has a job, poverty, the future gradually closing in, the silence of the evenings around the supper table, there's no place for passion in such a universe." (p. 97) However, his situation did not improve. Jeanne, his wife, must have suffered in silence. After several years, utterly wearied, she had resigned herself to leave him. "Joseph Grand in his turn had suffered. He could have made a fresh start, as Rieux reminded him. But there you are, he did not have the necessary faith. Only, he still thought of her. What he would have liked, was to write to her, justifying himself." (p. 98) The emotion that grips the poor man would invade us if the author had not fixed it in an unexpectedly grotesque image: "Grand blew his nose in a kind of checked napkin. Then he wiped his moustache." Rieux, it is laconically added, "gazed at him." (p. 98)

This confidential scene was to have, a few months later, a singularly pathetic heightening. Here are the facts. Grand, feeling the first symptoms of the disease, had gone to wander in the streets, "his features queerly contorted." Warned of this, Rieux had gone everywhere in search of him and had finally found him in tears, "almost glued to a window display of crudely carved wooden toys"—very like that Christmas shop in front of which had been decided his marriage with Jeanne. And he opens his heart again, but, the anguish of death projecting his old grief into an abyss of distress, he is hounded by the old desire to explain himself in a letter to Jeanne so that she could "be happy without remorse." Here, nothing any longer effaces the emotion. And if Rieux does not pronounce a word, his silence is a sufficiently explicit response: " . . . his tears overwhelmed Rieux because he could understand them and felt his own tears welling up. . . . This distress was his, and what wrung his heart at that moment was the passionate indignation a man feels when confronting the grief that all men share." (pp. 286-287)

We have said that Grand is the only character in the book possessing the consistency of a real hero of a novel.

First of all, this is true of him physically. "He was a man of about fifty years of age, tall and bent-shouldered, with thin arms and legs, and a yellowish moustache." (p. 29) Thus sketched from his entrance on the stage, when he seems to have only a walk-on part, this portrait will later be dwelt upon as to the main features, heightened as to colors by psychological and moral analysis. "At first sight, in effect, Joseph Grand was nothing more than *what he looked like, a humble municipal office worker.* Tall and thin, his clothes hung loosely upon him, being always too big, for he was under the illusion that, cut large, they would wear longer. Though he still had most of his lower teeth, he had lost those of the upper jaw, with the result that when his upper lip was raised in a smile, his mouth was a dark hole in his face. If we add to this portrait some additional characteristics—that he had the walk of a young seminarist, sidling along the walls and slipping into doorways, that he exuded the faint odor of smoke-filled basement rooms, that he had all the attributes of insignificance—it will be seen that *one could not imagine him anywhere except at an office desk,* studiously revising the tariff of the public baths or gathering together for a junior editor the materials for a report on the new garbage-collection tax. Even if not forewarned, you had the feeling that *he had been put into the world for the sole purpose of performing the*

*discreet but indispensable duties of a temporary assist-
ant municipal clerk* at sixty-two francs thirty centimes a
day. . . . In a certain sense, one might well say that his
life was exemplary. He was one of those men, rare in
our town as elsewhere, who always have the courage of
their good feelings. The little that he confided of himself
testified, in effect, to acts of kindness and a capacity for
affection that no one dares own to in our times." (pp. 56-
57, 59) We have purposely underlined three portions of
this passage: the author, it is evident, forestalls us in
judging of the unity of this individual: the perfect ade-
quacy of his physical aspect, social function and character confers upon him a real intensity of presence.

Psychologically, his "manias" finally render him unforgettable. "Rieux had already noted Grand's mania for
quoting the turns of speech common in his birthplace,
Montélimar, and following up with hackneyed expressions that came from nowhere, as for instance,
"divine weather," or "a magical effect." (p. 55) And
then, there is the mysterious literary work, that phrase
constantly rewritten: "One fine morning in May, a slim
horsewoman, mounted on a handsome chestnut mare,
was riding along the flowering bridle paths of the Bois
de Boulogne." Here again the profound unity of the
character is confirmed. There is not one situation in
which we are not made to remark that Grand "seemed to

search for words," that he "showed finickiness in the choice of expressions," that he "stammered," that "the words came stumbling out of his ill-furnished mouth," etc. It might be said that this infirmity finds, in the derisory ideal to which he is dedicated, a tragic prefer-ment. It has weighed upon his life like a fatality, bring-ing about a heartbreak of which he has not been cured. Because of this infirmity he has been unable to write the letter which would have set forth his rights to an ad-vancement; because of this infirmity, when his wife was growing weary of him, he was unable to "find the words which would have held her"; and again it is this infirmity which still keeps him from writing the letter which would justify him in the eyes of his beloved. Between these two impossible letters have been drawn on the chart of his life the curve of his destiny, the curve of his suffering. As we say of an actor, that he "fits his part," the fictional character, Joseph Grand, "fits" reality. Con-sidering the extent to which he seems to have impressed his very creator, it would not surprise us to learn that he was drawn from life.

Although revealed in a more subtle and insistent light, Joseph Grand plays only a small part, a little in the back-ground. He emerges from the shadows only to return, but we are given, in the moments when his face passes under the full light, a staggering glimpse of what the human vocation is, we experience it through him: it is a vocation of suffering and of humble grandeur. Although he fights the plague in his own way, by trying to establish correctly the statistics for the sanitary squads, Grand still remains absorbed in his own drama: the "slender horsewoman" of his literary efforts, and the memory of Jeanne, the two phantoms alternating in his nostalgic reveries. Between Rieux, who has unhesitatingly turned his back on personal happiness to throw himself wholeheartedly into the fight, and Rambert, who has joined it after a struggle with his conscience, Grand will represent that category of individuals who are impelled by a kind of sure and noble instinct to do what is necessary in time of misfortune, without any choice or renouncement on his part, and without any least displacement of the axis round which revolves their absurd, myopic world. ". . .The plague is here, we've got to defend ourselves, evidently. Oh, if everything was that simple!" And Grand, the narrator adds, "went back to his sentence." The reader cannot help smiling. The caricatural nature of the little man, whose pitiable ridiculousness is always underscored, goes beyond the merely picturesque and becomes charged with an important symbolical meaning. The "true healers," the "saints without God," emerge from the human flood and their noble faces, a little fixed in their expressions, risk giving to heroism an exceptional profile and a preeminence above happiness which the author, as we know, discountenances. But Grand's moustache, his "mouth like a dark hole," his round hat, his jumping-jack gesticulations, his sentimental moments, his manias prevent any hyperbolic interpretation. "Yes, if it's true that men like to hold up examples and types that they can call heroes, and if there must absolutely be some heroes in this story, the narrator commends to his readers this insignificant and obscure hero, who had to his credit only a little kind-heartedness and a seemingly ridiculous ideal." (p. 156)

Mediocre like that anonymous throng of people scourged by the Angel of the Plague "on the bloody threshing floor of pain," his heart crushed, Joseph Grand, beloved child of Camus, steps out of the rank and file to bear witness in his suffering and in his obscure courage to a dignity that the superior characters maintain in a clear-sighted revolt. It is to him, much more than to Rieux or Tarrou, that the narrative owes the best part of its optimism: *there are more things in men to admire than to despise.*

In short, the thought that emerges from *La Peste*, without disavowing the rather limited conclusions of *Le Mythe de Sisyphe*, marks the culmination of a theorizing on the absurd, extended to the certitude that "man, without the help of the Eternal or of rationalistic thought, can create, all by himself, his own values." (*Actuelles*, p. 111) Yes, the individual is the captive of an incomprehensible universe, against which his desire for coherence and his passion for justice miserably collide. Yes, his abandonment is irremediable, definitive, and the evil of which he is the prey is a pure absurdity. His sense of dignity commands him to reject this misfortune, which he shares with his fellow men; hence his revolt, but a revolt that postulates the greatest solidarity with his fellow men. Henceforth Sisyphus will no longer be alone; the stone he rolls will no longer be only his stone, and in the painful effort that he furnishes to push it up and immobilize it for a moment at the top of the hill (since the stone will fall down again, since the dead rats will reappear in the happy city), Sisyphus will perhaps approach that supreme gladness of soul in which his love will have gathered together all the joys of the world.

Paradoxically, this work, so magnificently optimistic, in which it is demonstrated that "a spontaneous appeal of his nature, an innate feeling of sympathy suffice to impel man towards grandeur,"[43] this work completely impregnated with charity and with a meaning understandable to Christians, is assuredly the most anti-

[43] Pierre-Henri Simon, *Témoins de l'Homme*, p. 192. Paris, 1951.

Christian of all the books of Camus. For it signally constitutes the work which aims to prove most clearly that man is in a position to edify, without God, a humanism of high nobility. Of such nobility that, at its highest, it approaches the realm of holiness. Moreover, humanism of this sort regards the Christian as an untrustworthy ally. Camus will always reproach the Father Paneloux who was capable of preaching that first sermon justifying the scourge and holding it up as divine punishment, thus subjecting man to sterile submission. The Father Paneloux of the second sermon, the one who, confronted with the death agony of a child, felt the collapse of his abstract concept of suffering, will always be reproached by Rieux for having abdicated his reason to preach a faith blindly consenting to evil, thus plunging into the hell of a completely Jansenist pessimism. "When an innocent boy can have his eyes put out," says Tarrou, "a Christian should lose his faith or consent to have his own eyes put out." (pp. 251-252)

By relying on the strength of the soul in adversity and exalting the purest values in man, Camus, in *La Peste*, invites us to put our bets on hope. We are made to see that the same ascetic grandeur is not within the reach of any and all; to those who prefer their personal happiness to it we are asked to give our understanding. But no matter how demanding this ethics may be, it cannot fail to attract those who, according to Albérès, "comprise the salt of the earth."

2. THE TRUE REVOLT

It is unlikely that the play *L'Etat de Siège*[44] would ever have been written or produced had not chance intervened. To quote from the program notes, it was first necessary for Jean-Louis Barrault to have "the idea of staging a play around the myth of the plague"— an idea dating from 1941—then, a few years later, for Albert Camus to "use the same myth in the writing of his novel," for him to be designated "quite naturally to Barrault as the desired collaborator." After that, the two had to come to an agreement as to the formula of such a play, "the avowed ambition of which is to mingle all the dramatic forms, from the lyrical monologue to the elements of the popular theatre, including mime, simple dialogue, farce, and chorus." The exceptional origin of this work explains why it represents, in the body of Camus' dramatic works, an exceptional aesthetic.

This play has been spoken of as a failure. True, the characters are pure abstractions endowed with mimicry and language; the dialogue is but a succession of a con-

[44] First performed on 27 October 1948 by the Company Madeleine Renaud-Jean-Louis Barrault at the Théâtre Marigny.

frontation of ideas; and the style is of a fabrication which does not always conceal its formulas. The sets, too, despite some touches of local color, are indeterminate and unreal, preeminently depicting a place where the imagination can conceive the unfolding of this imaginary story.[45] We are also willing to believe that no spectator was really moved by it. But such was not the author's ambition. "In short, it is a question of imagining a myth that might be intelligible to all spectators." (Program notes) In other words, the object was to set minds to thinking, not to set the tear-ducts working. And is it not also apparent to what point the allegorical type of the medieval morality play or the Spanish *"auto sacramental"* have served as inspiration for this intentionally dry stylization, this animated ideography wherein the beauty lies in the homogeneity of its movements, this multiform spectacle upon which are centered bright beams of thought?

That thought, fragmented in *La Peste*, comes together here, its elements fused and unified. In passing

[45] Which renders quite inopportune the accusations brought against the author by Gabriel Marcel in *Les Nouvelles Littéraires*, accusations founded essentially upon the fact that a play criticizing the totalitarian world should have its scene laid in Spain. Camus, in his reply, *"Pourquoi l'Espagne?"* ("Why Spain?") which was reprinted in *Actuelles* (pp. 241-250), shows that his work, although of general bearing, does not lack some historical justifications, even when it would seem to be directed against the Franco régime.

from the realm of the novel to the perspective of the stage, the themes of revolt are organized in a coherent pattern.

The plot may be summarized as follows. Above Cadiz, a comet has traced its baleful portent. The Plague, which has taken human form—and "the look of a noncommissioned officer"—is not long in putting in an appearance and setting up a dictatorship. This new master "does not rule; he judges." "His palace is a barracks, his hunting lodge is a law court. A state of siege is proclaimed." Immediately the stigmata of the disease appear on the flesh of the inhabitants; at the first faint indication, the victim is suspect; two indications, he is condemned; three, he is suppressed. Terror reigns, or rather functions, for everything is regulated, even death. Denouncements are encouraged, executions are massive, there are concentration camps, and none of this is left to chance. The all powerful machine of bureaucracy pitilessly crushes the palpitating flesh of life and liberty.

Diego alone succeeds in dominating his fear. He who at the first onsets of the scourge has assumed the mask of a physician of the plague, now snatches away the gags that had silenced the humiliated populace and does not rest until he has aroused them to revolt, in a great wave of pride and wrath. This, despite the efforts of his betrothed, Victoria, to hold him back for the sake of their love from this revolt which he had felt growing in him. But how keep alive personal happiness and at the same time do what must be done? Diego dedicates himself to the cause of humanity and from that derives his strength. He knows, however, that "it is a force that consumes all, leaving no room for happiness." Having looked the Plague in the face, he checks the murderous machine; but having dared to continue to face it, he will be struck down by the evil.

In the liberated town, thanks to his sacrifice, those who fled make their reentry, "The stodgy and optimistic and comfortable citizenry in the vanguard, as usual." Everything will begin again. Nada, the nihilist, the dark henchman of destruction, commits suicide, thus consummating the breakdown of a revolt against the absurd which has renounced taking root in love.

Rieux, in *La Peste,* neglected his personal happiness to defend the happiness of others; at the end, his wife and his friend Tarrou were dead. In *L'Etat de Siège* the sacrifice of the hero is supreme: Diego pays with his life. We may wonder if, in making the "honesty" of Diego conclusive by his martyrdom, Camus did not want to bring an additional thought to the message of *La Peste.* After having demonstrated what some men should and could accomplish for the happiness of all, he would specify that they cannot be permitted to have any least illusion as to their personal fate.

D. HOPE

1. AGAINST NIHILISM

Returning once more to the problem of murderous revolt, the author of *La Peste* had published in January 1948 a little essay entitled *Les Meurtriers délicats*.[46] In it there was a question of the organized attempt, in 1905, against the life of the Grand Duke Serge, by a group of terrorists belonging to the Socialist Revolutionary Party. In it could be seen how men of integrity, in revolt against a criminal society and necessarily brought to consent to crime, also made it their constant care "to leave contradictions behind and to create values which they lacked." To begin with, by gladly and willingly offering their own lives in payment for the lives of their victims, considering that the violence they disproved in the depths of their hearts—but to which it was impossible not to resort—could be justified by their personal sacrifice. Secondly, by the qualms of conscience they felt in connection with the lives of others, staying the execution of their plan from the

[46] In *La Table Ronde*, no. 1, Jan. 1948. This essay is taken up again in *L'Homme Révolté*, pp. 206-216.

moment that they risked compromising an innocent person, a "stranger." Thus the student Kaliayev renounced throwing the bomb at the carriage of the Grand Duke, because the intended victim was accompanied by his nephews.

LES JUSTES[47]

The story of this attempted assassination furnishes the main part of the action in the play *Les Justes* ("The Just"), as the author himself has made a point of saying in the Théâtre Hebertot's program: "In effect, extraordinary as some of the situations in this play may be, they are nonetheless historical. However, this does not mean, as will be shown, that *Les Justes* is a historical play. But all the characters really existed and conducted themselves as I relate it."[48]

Two protagonists confront each other: Stepan and Kaliayev. United in one action, they remain divided on the question of the principles that should inspire the action.

As for Stepan, only the revolution counts; he believes that dedicating himself to the liberation of the Russian people means recognizing all rights and being hindered neither by honor nor justice nor sentiment nor

[47] A play in five acts. Gallimard, 1950.
[48] Quoted by Robert de Luppé, in *Albert Camus,* 1952.

the murder of a child. Humiliated, bearing the marks of
the prison and the whip, Stepan in reality seeks in
revolutionary terrorism nothing but the assuagement
of his hatred. "Where would I find the strength to
love? But there remains to me at least the strength to
hate." At the very instant when his comrades are secretly
preparing to inflict death, his veritable and nihilistic
thought bursts out, and escapes in a cry of relief:
"There is too much to do; the world must be destroyed
from top to bottom!" Love cannot come until afterwards.

Quite the opposite, Kaliayev tries to maintain in the
midst of the claims of revolution the contradictory
claims of the heart. No, the revolution does not confer
upon revolutionaries every right! "Even in destruction,"
as Dora will remark, "there is an order, there are limits."
For instance, the life of innocents, the lives of the Grand
Duke's nephews. That day, we must remember, Kaliayev
will abstain. This will earn him a torrent of abuse from
Stepan, will cause him to be suspected of cowardice
and to be treated as a "poet" and a "softie." What matter! His feeling is that love cannot and should not have
to wait until afterwards! For it is in the name of his
love for his oppressed compatriots that Kaliayev fights
and accepts the risks of the gallows. It is in order that
this love may triumph today—and not tomorrow—over

the murder that he has agreed to administer justice, and not to assassinate. Hear him: "But as for me, I love those who live today on the same earth as I do, and they are the ones I salute. It is for them that I fight and that I agree to die. And for that city of the future, about which I am not sure, I would not engage to strike my brothers in the face. I will not add to living injustice for the sake of a dead justice." The second time, the Grand Duke being alone, Kaliayev throws the bomb.

From that time onward, Kaliayev expects nothing but the appeasement granted by death. His death will render all its retributive purity to his act; by dying, he will pay for the life he took; by dying, he will recover his innocence. So it is that when the Grand Duchess herself comes to the prison to assure him that she will intercede for him, he implores her to take no such step. He will be hanged.

This conflict, at the centre of which the rebel tries to size up the just act, and which is composed simultaneously of love and violence, in no way eclipses the conflict of the man torn between his egoistic desire for happiness and the heart-rending appeal for fraternity. After Rieux, after Rambert, after Diego, Dora and Kaliayev have turned their backs on love, for they, too, have had to recognize the inhuman vocation of "the just." "Yes, love is impossible, that is our lot." Impossible even, at the height of the conflict, to enjoy that moment of respite when they can forget, even for an hour, the atrocious misery of this world. In a word, impossible ever to relax. ". . . In summer, Yanek, do you remember? But no, it's always winter. We are not of this world, we are among the just. There is a warmth which is not for us. Oh, pity for the just!"

While Kaliayev, in a final thought as to the things that had warmed his life, could only conclude: "Those who love today must die together if they want to be reunited." Dora, for her part, has reached an identical conclusion. "It's so much easier to die of our own contradictions than to live them." Thus precisely the contradiction is resolved. Perhaps, in the fires of suffering, on the funeral pyre of the death sentence, love will survive, like the phoenix, at last reconciled to the passion for justice, for which it has immolated itself. From the depths of his cell, Kaliayev cannot keep himself from imagining that "rendezvous of grief." Dora, uplifted by a similar intuition, implores them to let her throw the bomb next time. The punishment to which they offer themselves not only sublimates their devotion to the cause of justice, but also redeems the evil to which they have consented in the name of that justice.

Thus are rejoined in them the feeling of guilt which consumed Tarrou in a purifying fire and that of solidarity which drew Rieux away from his personal happiness to make him assume the burden of others' suffering. In them are mingled the two types of rebels, the "true healers" and "the saints without God."

"The theme of happiness here receives an ultimate promotion. Kaliayev . . . recovers, beyond earthly pleasure, a kind of terrible happiness, a kind of 'wintry' love which unites him to his fellow men. In *Les Justes* we are far from the joys of sun and summer that are chanted in *Les Noces*. Here, Camus attempts a secular tranfiguration of the religion of happiness."[49]

Inspired by history as to the facts, *Les Justes* overflows the historical bounds in its significance. Here the past is not resuscitated for itself, but for the lesson of exigency it can give to the contemporary world issued from it and so tragically unfaithful to its example. In a brief letter of rectification addressed to the magazine *Caliban*,[50] the author emphasizes the topicality of the play: "The 'modern' reasoning, as they say, consists in settling the problem: If you do not want to be executioners, you are choirboys, and vice versa. Kaliayev, Dora Brillant, and their comrades, fifty years ago, refuted this base notion. Their message to us across the

[49] Charles Moeller, *op. cit.*, p. 70.
[50] *Caliban*, No. 39, May 1950, pp. 22-24. This reply, entitled "La Justice, elle aussi a ses pharisiens," is reprinted in *Actuelles II*, pp. 21-24.

years is that, on the contrary, there is a dead justice and
a living justice; and justice dies from the moment it
becomes a comfort, when it ceases to be a burning
reality, a demand upon oneself." The revolutionary
apostles of 1905, in their revolt which created new
values, call upon us to confront the nihilism and the
conformism of our time, which they proved to be monstrous forgeries of justice. We know Camus' undying
mistrust of all systems of ideas; he is too well aware
of the excesses to which those who insist upon any
kind of absolute can be carried. With *Les Justes* and the
exemplary intransigence of the protagonists' scruples,
he clears the ground for the unmasking of the political
ideologies of the century.

2. BEYOND NIHILISM

In order to appreciate *L'Homme Révolté*,[51] a compact
and recondite work, taut and concentrated in its
reasoning, we can do no better than quote an extract
from one of Camus' replies to the criticisms it aroused,
wherein the author explains himself. "All those people
for whom the problems aired in this book are not
merely theoretical have comprehended that I was
analyzing a contradiction which had at first been mine.
The thoughts of which I speak have nurtured me and I

[51] Paris, 1951. Published as *The Rebel* in New York, 1956.

wanted to carry them further by ridding them of what
I believe prevented them from advancing. I am not,
in effect, a philosopher, and I can speak only of what
I have experienced. I have experienced nihilism, contradiction, violence, and the vertigo of destruction. But
at the same time I have hailed creative powers and the
privilege of living. Nothing authorizes me to judge in
a detached way an epoch of which I am completely
a part. I judge it from within, merging myself with it.
But henceforth I reserve the right to tell what I know
about myself and others, on the sole condition that
what I say shall add nothing to the intolerable wretched-
ness of the world, but merely with the object of point-
ing out, within the dim imprisoning walls where we
are groping, the still visible points where doors may
open . . . I am interested only in a new renaissance."[52]

This work, then, represents, like the preceding ones,
and for the same reasons, a testimony to that line of
thought which we have followed step by step from its
awakening. It comprises a testimony that is decisive, *the*
testimony, rather, for Camus' system of thought here
culminates, achieves fulfillment and maturity.

It would therefore be a gross distortion of facts to

[52] Letter to *Libertaire*, reprinted in *Actuelles II*, pp. 77-84, under
the title, "Révolte et Romantisme."

regard *L'Homme Révolté* as a theoretical essay or a historical study of revolt. Though it is true that the history of revolt here occupies an important place, the ethical preoccupations of the author nonetheless conserve their preeminence. He warns us of it, moreover, on the threshold of the work: "Again, the important thing is not, as yet, to go to the root of things, but, the world being what it is, to know how to live in it." (p. 14)

We have seen how, throughout *La Peste*, the theme of revolt took precedence over the theme of the absurd, so original in *L'Etranger;* in the same way, the problem of suicide studied in *Le Mythe de Sisyphe* is here supplanted by the problem of murder. "This essay proposes, in the face of murder and revolt, to pursue a train of thought which began with suicide and the concept of the absurd." (p. 15) Such changes of illumination are natural and at the same time logical. It is natural that the experience of the man, informed by events, should in its turn mould the thought of the writer. "In the age of negation, it was of some avail to examine one's position relative to suicide. In the age of ideologies, we must examine our position relative to murder." (p. 14) It is logical that the two trains of thought should be systematized, the first being augmented and extended in the second.

L'HOMME RÉVOLTÉ (THE REBEL)

The introduction signalizes the harmony between these two trains of thought by a new analysis of the concept of the absurd, this time in its relation to murder.

The Absurd and Murder. The absurd attitude, defined in *Le Mythe de Sisyphe*, in no way bears upon murder. This indifference is tantamount to a consent or approbation, as though one were to say, "Nothing has meaning and the crimes committed around me have no more importance than all the rest: I allow them. Nothing has meaning and I want to act, to impose my will, to conquer; murder is useful to me, is opportune; I approve it."

Such an attitude, which endeavors to be, and indeed believes itself to be faithful to logic, cannot but betray a serious contradiction. We recall the reasoning by which suicide was rejected. "But it is obvious that the concept of the absurd admits that human life is the only necessary good since . . . without life, the absurdist wager would rest upon nothing." (p. 19) Then whoever endeavors to derive his rule of life from the absurdist doctrine ends up inevitably in nihilism while wearing himself out in contradictions. Camus denounces here the tragic error of our time. In effect, "the privileged emotion" which has bared the irrationality of the world and of our own lives cannot serve as a basis of action; it constitutes "nothing but a point of departure, a vivid criticism of life—the equivalent, on the plane of existence, of systematic doubt." (p. 21)

Consequently, we must go beyond the absurd, more exactly, we must be "caught up in the irresistible movement by which the absurd excels itself." This movement is revolt. The absurd has led us into an impasse; will revolt succeed in finding the reasons which should justify it? A preliminary examination of the content of revolt must be made. The first chapter, which gives the title to the essay, is devoted to this.

The rebel. A slave who suddenly rebels is affirming the existence of a limit beyond which he will not tolerate humiliation. He deems that a part of himself deserves to be respected and, by that very fact, "he proceeds to place it above everything else and proclaims it preferable to everything, even to life itself." In other words, he recognizes the transcendence of a *value* which not only surpasses himself but humanity entire.[53] "It is for

[53] At this point of the demonstration the occasion presents itself quite naturally to Camus to emphasize that he is not an existentialist, that for him the essence precedes existence: "Analysis of revolt leads at least to the supicion that, as the Greeks believed, but contrary to the postulates of contemporary thought, a human nature does exist." It is well to recall that already, in 1945, Camus, interviewed by Jeanine Delpech, spoke out clearly on this point: "Sartre and I both published all our books, without exception, before making each other's

the sake of everyone in the world that the slave asserts himself when he decides that a command has infringed on something within him which does not belong to him alone, but which is common ground where all men—the man who insults and oppresses him, even—have a natural community." (p. 28)

Thus, in rebelling, "man surpasses himself and identifies with others," since revolt implies the widest complicity. Conversely, human solidarity, at least in a universe closed to absolute values, does not assert itself except on the level of rebellion. From the moment that rebellion neglects or rejects or destroys this solidarity, it "loses simultaneously its right to be called rebellion." Therefore, a limit exists, which should always be kept in mind, constantly remembered. We must say No to the plague which engenders suffering, but Yes to life with its body being consumed by the plague; Yes to respect for humanity and at the same time No to the injustice of humanity. Without this "perpetual tension" between a Yes and a No, revolt degenerates, becomes acquiescence or murder. As absolute negation, revolt hands life over to the folly of anarchy, in which "every-

---

acquaintance. When we did meet it was to note at once our differences. Sartre is existentialist, and the only book of ideas that I have published, *Le Mythe de Sisyphe*, was directed against the philosophers called existentialists." (*Nouvelles Littéraires*, November 15, 1945.)

thing is permitted"; as absolute affirmation, revolt consecrates the apotheosis of evil and recognizes suffering
only to add to it. In the one case as in the other, it
assumes but one of the terms of its vocation and is faith-
less to itself.

There now remains for the author to confront the
conclusions of this analytical study with the works and
acts in which the spirit of revolt has been expressed. At
this point the author turns towards History, asking it to
bear witness. Principally he examines the history of our
time, because our secularized [*désacralisé*] age has made
rebellion "one of the essential dimensions of man." The
excesses of one rebellion can be explained, in part at
least, by the excesses of another. Hence, in passing in
review the various historical manifestations of rebellion,
"we shall have to say, each time, whether it remains
faithful to its first noble promise or if, through negli-
gence or folly, it forgets its original purpose and becomes swamped in tyranny or servitude." (pp. 35-36)

The investigation will take up first the rebellious
attitude as it is displayed in literature, on the plane
of thought, then the attitude which, turned into actions,
becomes embodied in revolutions. From metaphysical
rebellion (Chapter II) to historical rebellion (Chapter
III) we will follow the route which leads from the idea
to action.

Metaphysical rebellion. This "movement by which man protests against his condition and against all creation," is seen by Camus to have had its first expression with Epicurus, who figures as a forerunner whose influence can be felt in the "absolute negation" of Sade, the "dandies," Dostoyevsky, and in the "absolute affirmation" of Stirner and Nietzsche, ending in the "midnight exaltations" of the surrealists. With all these rebels, despite their particular attitudes, Camus finds the same "intemperance of the Absolute." And in either of the two types of rebellion, whether of total refusal or total acceptance of things-as-they-are, the revolt culminates in murder.

Historical rebellion. When rebellion, that "nostalgia for innocence," consents to be guilty and take up arms, it runs directly to murder and leads to revolution. The passage from the one to the other is subtly noted: "Rebellion, by its very nature, is limited in scope. It is no more than an incoherent statement. Revolution, on the other hand, originates in the realm of ideas. It is precisely the injection of ideas into historical experience, while rebellion is only the movement that leads from individual experience into the realm of ideas." (p. 136) Metaphysical rebellion accepts or precognizes the killing of others; revolution kills not only men but also principles. Thus, the regicides of 1793, with whom the history of modern revolutions begins, attacked in the person of the king the representative of God on earth, "yet even so, without daring to kill the Eternal Principle." The Reason which they substituted, and which inspired a religion of total virtue in Saint-Just, plunged them into the bloody night of the Terror.

After them came the *"déicides"* ("God-killers"), enthusiastic disciples of Hegel, whose dialectic, after having tried to destroy all transcendence utterly, had stirred in them the nostalgia for a divinity, but a terrestrial divinity. Whereas the reasonable absolute of Saint-Just and Rousseau soared above history, Hegel's identified itself with history. The values of truth and justice no longer vitalized action but had to be conquered by action; thus, they "ceased to be guides in order to become goals." It is easy to guess what the opportunistic or passionate proselytes of this dynamic philosophy were able to derive from it. "If nothing can be clearly understood before truth has finally been brought to light, then every action is arbitrary and force will finally reign." (p. 184) And murder will be installed as a provisional ethics. The time of individual terror and terrorism is inaugurated.

The action of the young Russian terrorists who, from 1820 to 1905, were to fling themselves, in the midst of the people's indifference, into an assault on tyranny, is to be written down to a prolongation of the German ideology of the nineteenth century, and composes in letters of blood the martyrology of the socialist revolution. Their outrages cannot make their sacrifices be forgotten. "Almost all of them paid for this liberation by suicide, execution, prison, or insanity." With these "squeamish assassins" (Camus' phrase is *"meurtriers délicats"*), rebellion triumphed for a moment over nihilism. But since its victory coincided with the death of its heroes, it was not long in betraying itself and returning to the infidelity that had so painfully been surmounted for a short while. And even, it "now contemplates the subjection of the entire universe." The despairing philanthropy of a Chigalev, possessed by the idea of equality, resignedly foretokened "the totalitarian theocrats of the twentieth century and State terrorism."

With the initial concept "that everything is meaningless and that history is only written in terms of the hazards of force," Hitler and Mussolini tried in vain to construct a universal empire based on State terrorism and irrational terror. Humiliated and full of hatred, they expected passion to give them what reason could not give. Hitler proclaimed the superiority of the future over the individual, thus plunging his people into a policy of endless conquest; as was required by the presence of perpetual enemies both within and without the State, creating perpetual terror, since the enemies would exist as long as the conquest was pursued. The State thus conceived could only be identified with an immense barracks inhabited by millions of silent slaves, and resounding with the imperious howls of a deified Fuehrer. "The commandments of the leader, posturing in the burning bush of spotlights, on a Sinai of planks and flags, therefore comprise both law and virtue. Suppose the superhuman microphones issue a single order for a crime to be committed: the criminal order is handed down from chief to subchief until it ultimately reaches the slave who receives orders without passing them on." (pp. 227-228) Propaganda or repressions within the walls, war outside the walls; the Empire of Efficiency was based on ruins and hecatombs. As for the Italian dictator, he announced "the exaltation of the dark powers of blood and instinct, the biological justification of the worst that the instinct for power produces" and founded his State on the absolute: "Nothing beyond the State, above the State, against the State. Everything to the State, for the State, in the State." (p. 227)

The dream of world-unification which was barely caressed by the Fascist mystics remained for Russian Communism to propose as a definite and incontestable aim, sustained by a metaphysical ambition and a doctrine with universal pretensions. The total revolution thus envisaged has, to date, been expressed "under the auspices of the rational State as it is to be found in Russia." Camus devotes no less than seventy pages to criticizing this State terrorism, so much more efficacious and solid than the State terrorism of the Fascists, because founded upon a rationale of terror.

To take over from that God killed by Hegel, then to set up the Religion of Humanity "unified in one immense army, one immense factory, no longer aware of anything but heroisms and inventions" (Julien Benda), to establish, in an absolute subjection to the material world and an exaltation of its powers, the imperialism of the human species, at last in command of creation—such was the ambition. As for the doctrine, it allowed itself to be defined by Karl Marx in a double prophecy, bourgeois and revolutionary. Bourgeois, because it prolonged the philosophy of progress current in the seventeenth and eighteenth centuries, crediting the scientific Utopia of Auguste Comte and borrowing from the economists of the industrial revolution certain essential features; revolutionary, through its theory of economic determinism and its prediction of a golden age in the future. All of which demands a word or two of explanation.

According to Marx, man and his thought are constantly and necessarily dependent upon the means of subsistence, therefore of production. That is to say, man, the founder of society, is thereby also created by society. In this double economic and social determinism, there is no room for any transcendence, even that of reason. History covers all, reigns over all, receives its movement from the class struggle. We know that with the advent of the nineteenth century, with the progress of the machine and the opening of international markets, the workers became more and more aware of being dispossessed of their means of production which were "concentrated in the hands of those able to buy." Bourgeois capitalism was making ready to devour everything. At this point the fatalistic prophecy of Marx intervened. According to him, capital would not stop growing, would not stop absorbing all small enterprises, concentrating in the hands of a few the wealth produced by the workers and stolen from their work. Ruined, the middle classes would swell the ranks of the proletariat. Thus, little by little, "an immense army of oppressed slaves find themselves confronting a handful of despicable masters." Then, what should happen would happen. Neither crises nor misery could be avoided. The proletariat, dragged to the very lowest, degraded and despoiled to the last degree, would "bring forth the supreme dignity from the supreme humiliation."

The universal revolution would break out, abolishing the shameful exploitation of man by man. Then, said Marx, "history, in a supreme act of violence, will cease to be violent."

Unfortunately it so happens that the facts have invalidated these economic predictions and "the proletariat has rejected the historical mission with which Marx had rightly charged it." The Bolshevik revolution, faced with other powers, found it necessary to be powerful itself. Like the capitalism which it aimed to abolish, the collectivity is forced "to arm and rearm, because others are arming and rearming. It does not stop accumulating and will never stop until the day when perhaps it will reign alone on earth. For that to happen, moreover, it must undergo a war." (p. 271) Is the radiant city of justice and reconciliation nothing, then, but a mirage? It would seem that even in the time of Lenin it could not be otherwise regarded. Lenin, laying the foundations of a military empire, had to juggle liberty progressively in the name of "the Kingdom of Ends," when "in a world finally subjected and purged of adversaries, the final iniquity will have been drowned in the blood of the just and the unjust." And Camus, after having exposed the plan from the affirmations of Lenin himself, proceeds to synthesize the opportunist movement which shapes its course to such a mystification: "From the rule of the masses and the concept of the proletarian revolution we move on to the idea of a revolution made and directed by professional agents. The ruthless criticism of the State is then reconciled with the necessary but provisional dictatorship of the proletariat, in the person of its leaders. Finally, it is announced that the end of this provisional condition cannot be foreseen and that, moreover, no one has ever dared to promise that there will be an end." (pp. 285-286) From this moment onward, the dream of universal liberty, requiring a total submission to history (which is to say, to Empire), reduces man to total slavery. His human nature denied, the individual summed up in the "social unit" and degraded to the rank of an object, dialogue and personal relations eliminated and replaced by propaganda or polemic, "the ration coupon substituted for bread; love and friendship submitted to the doctrine, and destiny to the plan; punishment considered the norm, and production substituted for living creation, quite accurately describe this disembodied Europe, peopled with phantoms, victorious or subjugated, of power." (p. 295)

But that is not all. In this totalitarian universe where, under cover of justice, are committed the worst injustices, we find the worst injustice of *the trial* superimposed. Every citizen is suspect and presumed guilty.

It is not enough for him to approve the régime, still less to be neutral (indifference is equivalent to hostility!), he must still be able constantly to prove that he has faith and lives according to that faith. "Consummating its history in its own way, the revolution is not content with killing all rebellion. It insists on holding every man, down to the most servile, responsible for the fact that rebellion ever existed and still exists under the sun." (p. 300)

"Here ends the surprising itinerary of Prometheus," writes Camus, fixing the transformations of historic revolution in the colorful imagery of myth. "Proclaiming his hatred of the gods and his love of mankind, he scornfully turns away from Zeus and approaches mortal men in order to lead them in an assault against the heavens. But men are weak or cowardly; they must be organized. They love pleasure and immediate happiness; they must be taught to refuse, in order to grow up, must be given immediate rewards. Thus Prometheus, in his turn, becomes a master who first teaches, then commands. The fight is prolonged and becomes exhausting. Men doubt that they can safely approach the city of light and doubt even if the city exists. They must be saved from themselves. The hero then tells them that he, and he alone, knows the city. Those who doubt of its existence will be cast out into the desert, chained to a rock, offered as food to the vultures. The others will henceforth march in darkness, behind the pensive and solitary master. Prometheus alone has become god and reigns over the solitude of men. But he has won from Zeus only solitude and cruelty; he is no longer Prometheus, he is Caesar. The real, the eternal Prometheus has now assumed the aspect of one of his victims. The same cry, springing from the depths of time, resounds forever through the Scythian desert." (p. 301)

But now the author finds it is time to reach some positive conclusions. The fifth chapter, "Thought at the Meridian," with its thirty-five pages, perhaps weighs very lightly, as someone has remarked, in comparison with the negative section which constitutes more than two thirds of the work. But this is to forget that the description of error, treason, and darkness carries within it the force of truth, fidelity and light, and that once the roads to inferno are denounced, the road to Damascus lies open without need for comment.

Rebellion and murder. By the time we have investigated history, it appears that rebellion, in having recourse to murder, condemns itself to illogicality, exactly as does the doctrine of the absurd. "From the moment he strikes, the rebel cuts the world in two. He rebelled in the name of the identity of man with man and he sacrifices the identity by consecrating the difference in blood. His very being, in the midst of suffering and oppression, was contained in this identity. The same movement which aimed at affirming him thus brings an end to his existence." (p. 348)

In "the nihilistic murder," the rebel recognizes no limit to his action; whenever he rebels to vindicate the liberty of all, he proves, with weapon in hand, that he refuses liberty to his victim, which is to say that, in the long run, he refuses it to all. "Nihilistic passion, adding to injustice and lies, destroys in its fury its original existence and thus abolishes the most cogent reasons for revolt." (p. 352)

On the plane of history and in the absence of all values of a superior order, rebellion is caught between irreconcilable principles: violence and nonviolence, justice and liberty. The efficacity of the act "presupposes the cynicism of violence"; renouncement of violence reduces us to acquiescence in slavery. These two opposed attitudes unite in the same treason of revolt, in the same nihilism. Similarly, rebellion for the sake of justice, tolerating no contradiction, suppresses all liberty, while absolute liberty, establishing "the right of the strongest to dominate," maintains and confirms the reign of injustice. In reality, the paradoxes in which revolutionary action becomes involved do not exist except in the mind fascinated by the absolute and abstracted from reality. As the author reminds us, in having recourse to the allegorical expression "the representatives on earth" of such people are "effectively, the yogi and the commissar." The yogi, lost in the mirage of a supernatural justice, turns away from rebellion and rejects reality. The commissar, on the contrary, admits only the facts of history, taken in its universality as a value susceptible of founding an ethic, a pure Utopia. Because history is not completed and its veritable meaning cannot be clarified except in its totality at the end of its career. Because, especially, we are powerless to have a global grasp of a reality in which we are integrated, powerless to survey at a glance a whole of which we are a part. "Historical murder," in its chimerical appetite for the absolute—absolute rationalism or absolute nihilism —distorts the rebellion it seeks to make triumphant. A revolutionary act which wishes to be coherent in terms of its origins should actively consent to the relative and thus express fidelity to human conditions. A relative justice. The revolutionary must know that man is incapable of absolute virtue, but also that evil can be combatted, that it is possible at least to attempt not to be its accomplice. He understands that justice does not exist without freedom or freedom without justice; that at all costs the two ideas "must find their limits in each other" if he would "preserve the common existence that justifies the insurrection." Such limitation would forever prevent violence from "negatively founding servitude and a régime of violence." If, nevertheless, recourse to violence cannot be avoided, when facing an excess of injustice, for example, the revolt must maintain its ties with "a personal responsibility and an immediate risk." The rebel engaged in an "authentic revolt will only consent to take up arms for institutions that limit violence, not for those which codify it." (p. 360)

Before defining this attitude in politics, Camus ponders the question, "Is rebellion efficacious?" and replies, "It is the only attitude that is efficacious today." In a classic use of language, he opposes the word "efficacity" (of a creative revolt) to the "efficiency" that historical absolutism derives from the terror and silence of its "desert." We are to understand that the results expected of an "efficacious" revolt should mark a victory over injustice and tyranny, rendering it intransigent as to the choice of "the means," while the second, essentially aiming only at its own triumph, cares little for moral ethics, provided it succeeds, and will authorize itself to have recourse to *any* and *every* means. On the one hand, action is self-disciplined because of the grandeur of the objects it pursues. On the other hand, these same objects serve as pretexts for permitting any act that will impose them with certainty. No doubt, the action contained within the bounds imposed by respect for freedom and a sense of justice runs the risk of failing and of being destroyed. But if revolutionary action renounces this risk, the guarantees with which it sought to surround itself can only be forged in lies, dissimulation, cynicism, in short, its own negation.

Moderation and excess. The recognition of a limit, of "a mediating value," balances and maintains the contradictions of revolt, transfiguring it and enabling it to accomplish its true human dimensions. "In effect, there is a natural moderation in matter as well as in man," a moderation confirmed by science and material forces themselves. It is the excess of our epoch that has upset the movement of history. "Moderation, confronting this irregularity, teaches us that one part of realism is necessary to every ethic; that unadulterated virtue is homicidal; and that one part of ethics is necessary to all realism; cynicism is homicidal." (p. 366)

There remains to be ascertained how this free and moderate attitude can become a part of history, and in what form of activity it can find its expression. Camus sees it realized in what is usually called revolutionary trade-unionism, which sprang from the very midst of reality—professional employment. Its efficacity has been proved. "It is this movement which, within a century, has enormously improved conditions of the working classes, taking them from the sixteen-hour day to the forty-hour week." (p. 367) But when the absolutist revolution seized upon this living reality to raise its protest, the very impetus of the revolt was broken, moderation was left behind, the counterpoise of argument was lost, resulting in an inevitable plunge into terror and murder.

Beyond nihilism. Let us pause a moment. It is important to realize that the essayist's train of thought, which we have now summarized, has neither this dry-as-dust aspect nor this stiff and labored manner. On the contrary, Camus employs, with sure and confident ease, a rich but close-knit phraseology which improves constantly upon itself. We cannot give an exact idea of this entire fifth chapter of the book without making it clear that the author leads up to his unique thought in a continual movement of confrontation. Gradually, the definition of true rebellion emerges, pictured clearly, pointed up by the corresponding critique of rebellion unfaithful to its origins. Near the conclusion, on the tenth page from the end of the book, the author gives free rein to his dialectics, releasing the lucid passion which had held it in check until then. For by this time he has touched the fundamentals of the problem and recognized that the triumphs of his reasoning partake of the antique wisdom, a heritage neglected by the

Occident to its loss. In the course of the essay he has also convinced himself that the real conflict of the century is the conflict "between German dreams and Mediterranean tradition, between the violence of eternal adolescence and virile strength, between nostalgia, rendered more poignant by knowledge and by books, and courage hardened and enlightened in the experiences of life." It is, moreover, a conflict to which the Christian Church has not remained foreign, since it "forsook its sunny Mediterranean heritage," neglecting nature to lay claims to temporal power and historical dynamism.

Thus the author, approaching his fortieth year, and as he rounds out his intellectual adventure, finds again that two-sided truth which, as a boy on the shores of North Africa, had been like the surge of his blood, but now elucidated, confirmed, founded in reason. And the poet who wrote *Les Noces*, strengthened by thought, takes up his song again in an assured voice to recount his triumph over midnight shadows and his hope of a renaissance; to tell of "the strange form of love" which animates his revolt, preoccupied with present happiness rather than with a far-distant and problematic Eden; to assert the extent of his refusal, while conscious of the permanence of evil, but also of the power of man "to diminish it arithmetically," and of his duty to "rectify in creation everything that can be rectified."

L'Eté[54]

"The work of Albert Camus," notes Pierre Néraud de Boisdeffre,[55] "would have been a hymn to happiness if it could have developed along the lines it followed originally; it would have celebrated man's nuptials with the unsullied earth, would have celebrated a world in which friendship is natural, where man's work is a vocation, where culture is a privilege, a world of which history has not yet taken possession." As a matter of fact, Camus has never stopped composing this hymn throughout the long Odyssey which, after a period of exile in the dark swamps of nihilism, was to bring him back to the smooth shores of Ithaca, "the faithful earth, the audacious and frugal thought."

Camus, heir of Greece, child of sea and sun, was torn by the war from his contemplation, and took his place "in the shuffling line of men standing before the open door of Hell." But even while fighting in those lurid shadows against the horror of a monstrous epos, and while denouncing "the capitals of crime" where the crushed silence of the enslaved was punctuated from time to time by the crepitation of the twelve blind

[54] *L'Eté*, collected essays. Published by Gallimard, 1954.
[55] "Débats: L'Homme Révolté de Camus," in *Psychologie moderne et réflexion chrétienne*, p. 217. Arthème Fayard, cahier No. 3, January, 1953.

bullets, he could not keep from singing, in his heart, a muted accompaniment to the millennial voices of trees and sky, a song celebrating happiness and beauty.

The eight essays gathered together in the volume entitled *L'Eté*—"Summer"—were composed over a period of almost fifteen years, between 1939 and 1953, and they leave no doubt as to this hidden but intense fidelity of the author to the tradition of his native land; a tradition of sunlight and moderation, a land where the sensation of living is so keen, so palpable, that it overwhelms us and reduces us to silence.

The thought of Albert Camus is not carried further by these essays; indeed, most of them appeared throughout the years in various magazines or anthologies. Certainly his logic of revolt is not extended. What these essays express is the inherent accord between this Mediterranean man and the land that gave him birth. We suddenly perceive that this North African who came among us in quest of a solution to the tragedy of the century has never really left his native shores; rather, they have never let him go. He eluded, for a time, the enchantment of the natural world in which he had grown to manhood, but never freed himself wholly from it. We may well admire and wonder when we note how, without failing in its severity, his rhetoric has been able at times to develop according to the throbbing of that nostalgia; as though a Descartes, without being false to himself, had allowed or even summoned a Chateaubriand to take the pen.

Among so many superbly written pages, we will select a few in which the poet has concentrated upon a seductive image. For example, this page in *Les Amandiers:* "When I lived in Algiers, I always waited patiently throughout the winter, because I knew that on one night, one single, pure, cold night in February, the almond trees of the Consuls Valley would cover themselves with white flowers. I marvelled, then, at seeing how that fragile snow resisted all the rains and the winds from the sea. Yet every year they endured, exactly the time required to prepare the fruit." (p. 73) What a marvellous act of faith, and what exorcism! At a time when the sword was again making an attack upon the Spring, when History was again threatening to subdue the spirit, that was how the memory of the land elected by the gods continued to glow against the darkness of despair. Camus was aware of it: ". . . sometimes, when the burden of life becomes too heavy in this Europe still full of misery, I turn my mind back towards those shining lands where so much force of eternal youth is still intact." (pp. 73-74) This secret force of eternal youth and innocence, this force of character which upholds the beautiful, hard, blue sky, is what "in the winter of the world, will prepare the fruit." The essay dates from 1940. The "meridian thought" already shines here and the man who declares that he does not sufficiently believe "in reason to subscribe to progress or to any philosophy of history" is already, here, a clear-seeing rebel, determined and mature. *Les Amandiers* contains "the certitude of the ever-returning sap."

These pages add nothing to the thought of Albert Camus, but when we discover in them that his mind has never ceased "to cultivate, within the bounds of ineluctable dangers the field of life, loved for itself, for all the rich treasures in which life abounds"[56] his thought is made secretly more tangible, is brought closer to us.

However, these essays risk disappointing those people who have made an effort to see in Camus' writings the work of a philosopher—despite his warnings. For they emphasize, by prolonging them as in a pause of music, the poetic chords with which *L'Homme Révolté* ends. Never has "the meridian thought" more openly revealed the affective substrata of Camus' nature, where everything is founded upon his sentimental adherence to the glittering land where he had the good fortune to be born. Let us quote a second time the essayist's frank avowal: "In effect, I am not a philosopher, I only know

[56] André Rousseaux, "L'Eté d'Albert Camus," *Le Figaro Littéraire*, March 20, 1954.

how to talk about the things I have experienced." It is in this quite personal (and consequently quite relative) perspective that we are invited to discover Camus' line of thought and judge it; indeed, to judge it according to any other criteria would be not only to betray but to negate it by emptying out its living sap.

An inclusive examination of the author's work, one not analytical like this present essay, which is centred upon the ideological and moral evolution that can be noted, would disclose the duality of the experience which has led us from *Les Noces* to *L'Eté*, passing by way of *Le Mythe de Sisyphe* and *L'Homme Révolté*. A lyrical experience to start with, during which his mind is fecundated in a privileged emotion; then an attempt to elaborate in thought the emotive seeds thus garnered. Here is a definite example which allows us to lay a finger on the transition from one creative attitude to the other. In *La Peste*, it is the spectacle of individual or collective suffering which unleashes sympathy and the feeling of solidarity; in *L'Homme Révolté* (which, in sum, only reduces to dialectic terms the symbolism of the novel), the feeling of solidarity takes shape and affirms itself in the movement of revolt. Robert de Luppé, who has noted this difference, asks, "But is not the profounder reality to be found in the novel?

Does not the direct vision of suffering awaken the conscience more than the actual revolt?"[57] No doubt, but the theoretical essay obeys the impulse which governs the findings of sensitive experience and reconstructs them according to an architecture that does not disdain a certain geometry. The feeling of duality, of ambivalence which characterizes Mediterranean thought, as Gabriel Audision has so well shown in his *Ulysse ou l'Intelligence,* constantly asserts itself in the writings of Camus, in strong contrast with his line of thought. Exaltation of life and humiliation of death, taste for happiness and appeal of fraternity, revolt and love, acceptance and refusal. And finally the coexistence in the very midst of his artist's vocation, of a tendency to lyricism and a need to dominate this tendency by thought; this alternance of song and rhetoric, of passionate warmth and cold reasoning is surely not without its significance.

Let it be said in passing, and with the aim of correcting an intolerable optical illusion, that nothing in his quality as a man or his personality as a writer relates him to Jean-Paul Sartre, Doctor of Philosophy, creator of a coherent doctrine, esoteric on certain points, and whose postulates furnish the armor of his entire body

[57] Robert de Luppé, *op. cit.,* p. 86.

of literary work, instead of testifying, as with Camus and Malraux, to adventures that have been lived.

To return to the double experience, lyrical and intellectual, of Camus, we should note that this internal disparity does not always flow in two distinct streams, but entails corresponding differences in the nature of his books and in their achievements. Thus, some of the constructions, as for instance *Le Malentendu* and *L'Etat de Siège,* show marks of the effort of adaptation to a theoretical pattern. *Le Mythe de Sisyphe* betrays a straining for stoical inflexibility; and *L'Homme Révolté,* despite some pages of soaring inspiration, at times shows painful constraint. On the other hand, the hymn to the beauty of the world comprised by *Noces* and *L'Eté,* the muted yet strong and virile recitative that is *La Peste,* the cry of purity and love that is *Les Justes* echo in us with an intensity of accent that only an authentic inspiration can sustain.

In sum, we would like to remind those who refuse the ultimate title of thinker to this rebel, that a tree is not judged by its roots, and that this tree of "solar truth," shimmering though it be and streaming with the warmth and sea spray that favored its growth, may very well be the truth of the new Renaissance which the best minds of our time do not despair of shaping.

E. REDISCOVERIES

After *L'Homme Révolté*, in which the balanced "Thought at the Meridian" seemed to be a kind of conclusion, or at least a culmination of the thought analyzed up to now; after *L'Eté*, the lyricism of which had but improved upon the accents of *Noces* with steadfast constancy; after this phase of activity lasting close to twenty years and which suddenly returns to its poetical source, as if to measure the distance run, it is legitimate to look questioningly into the future career of Albert Camus.

We know that he considers his work as barely begun and deems it primarily as but a necessary settling of matters between the century and the rôle he feels called upon to play in it. First of all, he wanted to "get in line" with his epoch ("*se mettre en règle avec*" are his words). The proof of his artistry could only come afterwards.

Thus, the period of criticism having been passed, his taste for a freer creativity begins to reassert its fragile and difficult demands.

Does this mean that the works to come—works of art rather than declarations of faith—will resolutely turn away from the problems of the hour? Not at all. But instead of deferring to them in his writings, Camus will do his utmost to dominate them, and instead of allowing them to dictate the substance and form of his works, will shape them to his needs. History, which provoked the virile retort that was *La Peste* and the sound demystification that was *L'Homme Révolté,* will no longer determine the inspiration of the creator, but will let itself be absorbed in his great effort to tap the tree of life. Henceforth the question of myth sinks into the background, giving way to the author's search for eternal truth, without, however, the one being necessarily immaterial to the other.[58]

"By one of those departures which are an indication of the originality and authenticity of his revolt, Camus evidently means to escape from the Manichaeism in which some critics would have confined him, and rediscover existence in all its living complexity."[59]

La Chute (The Fall)[60]

This short narrative of 170 pages, like *L'Etranger,* with which, rightly or wrongly, certain affinities have

[58] See: *Gazette de Lausanne,* March 28, 1954.

[59] Roger Quilliot, *La Mer et les Prisons* p. 268, (Essay on Albert Camus, published by Gullimard, Paris, 1956).

[60] Published by Gallimard, Paris, 1956. In its English translation, *The Fall,* published by Alfred A. Knopf, New York, 1957.

been discovered, has been variously received and understood by the critics. There has been unanimity on but one point: the quality of its composition and style. Once more Camus has been hailed as an incomparable artist,[61] assuredly one of the most rigorous and gifted of contemporary writers.

In effect, it is impossible not to be charmed by this long monologue which from the first page sues for our attention in a language that is marvellously pure, sometimes distant and slightly ceremonious, sometimes warmly familiar or stingingly sarcastic, sometimes eloquent, persuasive, and sometimes uplifted by a poetic imagination of infallibly clear vision. As P.-H. Simon has put it, we could hardly "resist the charm of this narration which is dry without baldness, rapid without excessive tension, illuminated with percussive formulas, in a tone of humor that is sometimes slightly grating but more often of a luminous and biting irony: the idea, scoured and polished, shines like a steel blade."

The monologist, who has broken with his past, lives under the false name of Jean-Baptiste Clamence in the

[61] "The writer has increased his marvels and multiplied his enchantments. His prose remains the most luminous and precise that we have read since the first works of Montherlant (but without Montherlant's arrogance or rhetoric), since the first works of Gide, even, (but without Gide's damp exudations of seduction), and the moralist has sharpened some unalterable aphorisms."—Alain Bosquet, in *Combat*, May 31, 1956.

slum quarters of Amsterdam, where he has taken to frequenting the seamen's bars along the Zeedijk, particularly the bar called Mexico-City; it is there that he watches out for the occasion to force the person at the next table, preferably a foreigner and a bourgeois—on this occasion a Frenchman, like himself—to open up the conversation so that he may disclose the secret of his clandestine existence, the reasons for his "fall."

The confession soon becomes something of a methodical introspection, and what we are asked to hear is not the story of a life but the adventures of a conscience. Furthermore, a complete background of bitter allusions to the cynicism of our epoch tends to efface the too personal elements existing in the case described.

It is, then, a confession, but a "calculated" confession, in which the anecdote goes beyond its particular reference to reach the human species through the individual and unmask man's deepest nature. In short, it is humanity entire that confesses through the mouth of this curious penitent; "the mirror into which he gazes, he finally holds up to others."

A *"calculated"* confession. A few years previously, Jean-Baptiste Clamence was a brilliant lawyer in Paris, a lawyer who championed noble causes, a defender of "widows and orphans."

Professionally, he experienced a comforting pleasure

in realizing that he was "on the right side." He felt himself above the judges, not having to judge, and above the accused, not being in the situation of being judged. He disdained the former and forced recognition from the latter; in a word, he soared. In his personal life he had been no less favored: good-looking, excellent dancer, fine talker, generous and courteous citizen, he enjoyed everywhere the same success and everywhere excelled. Such constancy in achievement, the apparent consummation of happy natural dispositions, inclined him to consider himself as "designated" for happiness, as "authorized for this happiness by some kind of superior decree." And yet, "always gratified, never sated," he was at the same time not satisfied with anything.

One evening, as night descended, very contented with his day, while lingering on a bridge over the Seine, the Pont des Arts, "his heart swelling with an enormous feeling of power . . . and of completeness," he had heard the sound of laughter behind him. He turned, saw no one, and as the sound diminished, "which had come from nowhere, if not the water," he was pervaded with a distress that it took some time to overcome.

In fact, he was never able to rid himself of that distress. His tranquil sufficiency had been shaken, his conscience had been awakened. He was about to see clearly within himself and discover his vanity, the sole impetus and end of his behavior: "the I-I-I." Until then, everything that was not his paltry person or did not concern it immediately, had "slid off" him and sunk into oblivion. Searching his memory, he recollected certain things that his introspection now revealed to him as being of overwhelming significance. To begin with, there was that memory of an altercation he had had, in the course of which he had been struck by an unknown person, without retaliating; an incident that had filled him with "sweet dreams of revenge." Then, there were the souvenirs of his multiple affairs with women, his comedian's skill in the game of seduction, his tyrannical egotism, memories of the only love he had ever experienced in all those adventures—and which was dedicated to himself. Finally, there was the most painful memory, of that woman who had thrown herself into the river from the Pont Royal, just after he had passed her, and whose desperate cry for help he had heard, without moving a muscle.

Thus, from memory to memory, and through a self-examination of constantly greater depth, Clamence was not long in bringing to light "the fundamental duplicity of human beings" and of comprehending that modesty helped him "to shine, humility to conquer, and virtue to oppress." At that moment, obsessed by the spectre of death, he was overwhelmed with a kind of vertigo at the thought that if he disappeared no one would ever know the truth about him. Time pressed, he could no longer disregard who he was—neither as to his lies nor his guilt. "To reveal to the eyes of the world the stuff I was made of, I wanted to break the handsome wax figure I presented everywhere." (p. 109) He decided to cover himself systematically with ridicule, which was a way of immunizing himself against the laughter he felt hovering about him. But his exhibitions of sincerity were taken to be pure eccentricities, and his remarks interpreted as "charming pleasantries." No one took him seriously.

He had recourse to women and naturally fell into his past errors. Incapable of great love, incapable of chastity, he but added to his sins, and his suffering became ever more acute. Whereupon he plunged into debauchery: alcohol and prostitutes. There, no hypocrisy, no play-acting, no obligation: a slow anaesthesia of the conscience. "I lived in a kind of fog in which the laughter became so muffled that I ended up by not noticing it any more." (p. 123) Was it the expected appeasement, the deliverance, the cure? Clamence could have hoped so, had not his nocturnal excesses obliged him to resume a more normal existence. But finally, his senses were blunted, his vitality weakened, his lucidity dimmed. "There was nothing more to do but grow old."

Alas, during a cruise, the sight of a floating débris not far from the liner disturbed him and revived the memory of the woman drowned near the Pont Royal. The cry for help from which he had turned away remounted from the depths of his memory. He realized, then, the permanence of his disorder, and his incurable blight. So then, he must accommodate himself to it, must "live in the dungeon called 'little-ease,'" with the stabbing pain of desire for innocence crushed beneath the weight of a guilty conscience.

On the point of concluding his story, Jean-Baptiste Clamence makes a surprising revelation to his interlocutor when he asks him to take a painting out of one of his cupboards. The painting is the missing panel from the Van Eyck "Mystery of the Lamb" altar-piece in the Ghent Cathedral of Saint-Bavon; it is the panel entitled "The Righteous Judges" that was stolen in 1934. A customer of the Mexico-City bar had sold it, one drunken night, for a bottle of wine, and the barkeep had hung it over the counter at first, but when told by Clamence where it came from he had finally deemed it more prudent to entrust it to the keeping of our ex-lawyer.

Stolen goods of inestimable worth, a worth which to Clamence has become exclusively symbolical. This affair of "The Righteous Judges" being henceforth prevented from adoring the Lamb of God, illustrated the definitive separation of justice from innocence. Did not this suggest a solution to his quandary? The only way to escape laughter reverted to managing things so that everyone would be subjected to it. Well, since no one was pure enough to dare to judge others without exposing himself to be judged, "one had to overwhelm oneself to have the right to judge others." Since every judge ends up one day as a penitent, "one had to travel the road in the opposite direction and practice the profession of penitent in order to end up as a judge." (pp. 159-160)

This function of judge-penitent to which, since then, he has dedicated himself, is exercised by Clamence according to a settled technique: "Covered with ashes, tearing out my hair by slow degrees, clawing my face with my own nails, but with eyes clear and penetrating, I stand before all humanity, recapitulating my causes for shame, without losing sight of the effect I produce, and saying, 'I was the lowest of the low.' Then, imperceptibly, I go on from the 'I' to the 'we.' And when I reach the 'This is what we are,' the trick has been played and I can tell them some home truths. Of course, I am like them; we're in the same boat. However, I have one superiority, I know what I am and this gives me the right to speak. I'm sure you see the advantage. The more I accuse myself, the more I have the right to judge you. Better still, I make you judge yourself and am relieved of the burden to that extent." (p. 162)

From that moment onward, the duplicity which yesterday was unendurable becomes comforting and one settles into it as into a state of happiness. The penitent, having become judge of those who, surprised at judging him, are induced, or "oriented" by his dissertation to become penitents themselves, again dominates and judges and rules. "What rapture to feel like God the Father and hand out definitive certificates of bad conduct and behavior!" (p. 165) No longer is there any question of changing one's existence. What good would it do, since infamy is general and one retains the prestige of having been the first to denounce it in oneself? "Only, the confession of my faults allows me to begin again with a lighter heart and to taste a double enjoyment, first of all in my nature, and secondly in a delightful repentance." (p. 164) Unexpected resolution, in which the rejection of evil savagely disintegrates and yields to it. But is Clamence sincere, and in displaying this triumphant cynicism is he not hardening himself against the secret awareness of being still helplessly cornered in the impasse from which he thought he had escaped?

Needless to say that in such an outline, though we

have given an idea of the logical content of the book, we have not given its affective tone. Yet the narrative touches us not only by what it confesses but also by the atmosphere in which the confessions are made.[62] And that atmosphere is diffused with consummate art not only by the intimations of the stage-setting but also by the character of the protagonist and the hidden fires of his words.

The setting. As we have seen, the setting is an important element in the symbolical aesthetics of Camus and participates in the drama of his previous myths. "The moral message included in a narrative by Camus is meant to be conveyed to us as an evocation. In a way, this type of book, with its ability to render us sensitive to what it means to communicate, partakes of the qualities of a prose poem more than of a novel."[63]

For the first time, the enchantments of the Mediterranean region, its light, sky, and sea, have not been convoked. A passing allusion is made to Greece, to note the demand of purity it makes upon its chosen ones. Quite the contrary, in this book where a conscience plumbs the depths of its impurity, where the mire is stirred up with cruel intensity, the desolate landscape

[62] ". . . he is not the artist who speaks, but who causes to speak."— Albert Camus, "Lettre au sujet du *Parti Pris*," in *Nouvelle N.R.F.*, Sept. 1956.

[63] André Rousseaux, in *Le Figaro Littéraire*, May 26, 1956.

of the Last Judgment was needed. And what could have been more suitable than this landscape of concentric canals that compose Amsterdam with its "breath of stagnant waters," this "immense Holy-water font" of the Zuider Zee; what could be better than this cold, clinical, sterilized light? "Just look at that heap of ashes on our left—they call it a dune, here; just notice the grey dike to our right, the ghastly beach below us, and in front of us the thin swill that is the sea, and the vast sky reflecting the pale waters. A soggy inferno, really; nothing but horizontals, no glitter; space is colorless, life at a standstill. Isn't this universal obliteration a vision of nothingness?" (p. 86)

The judge-penitent has not chosen his retreat by chance. With a very keen sense of stage-setting, he has understood that "the most beautiful of negative landscapes" will add to the upward movement of his confession and will destroy in others any slight inclination to withhold their own.

But at the very moment when he declares he is happy, reigning "at the zenith of the Netherlands sky" over this wilderness of mists, his nostalgia for the privileged lands of innocence wrings his heart: "Oh, sun, sands, and islands beneath the trade-winds, Oh youth, of which memory despairs!" (p. 166) And this cry—it is again as always the young North African who reasserts himself—reveals to us, beneath its rhetorical wrappings, the unavowed hurt of the protagonist.

The protagonist. Intelligent, lucid, a gifted talker, Clamence plays a part, or rather improvises it. He is simultaneously the one who talks, the one who listens to himself talk, the one who thinks only when talking, the one who talks without thinking, the one exalted by an image, depressed by a memory, stirred, slowed down, disoriented, or stimulated by the reactions of his interlocutor, or simply inspired by a feature of the landscape. In short, he is alive.

What he has to say does not constitute a report, his investigation does not comprise an inventory. He is not soothing his conscience, he is trying to persuade himself that he has soothed it. He calls his confession "calculated," his discourse "oriented"; he believes he is saying nothing but what he judges opportune to say and in a suitable manner. But the phrases escape him. He notices it sometimes and makes excuses: ". . . it's an overflow; the minute I open my mouth words flow out . . ." or else: "But I'm letting myself go, I'm pleading a cause!" or again: "Well now, I'm getting excited, I'm overdoing it." And warn us though he will, "Don't pay too much attention to my emotional outbursts or my ravings; they're controlled," we are not fooled and we understand that he is trying to cover up a moment of unconstraint or distraction by this pretence. At times his words stimulate his mind, force him to elaborate his turns of speech, giving us the impression of hearing the narrator think aloud; at times the confession is hurried or becomes arrested at a certain altitude, then, either losing momentum or slackening, it drops into anecdote; at times it slows down when the avowal becomes difficult, and remains suspended; and finally, at times, it throws off all constraint and pours out in an abstruse soliloquy or launches towards apocalyptic heights.

In truth, Clamence remains prime listener of Clamence. He reacts to his self-accusation and his penitent's lucidity is several times thwarted by the pain it causes him. We are made all the more aware of this suffering by the physical depression which progressively overwhelms him. On the fifth and last day of this painful "voyage to the limits of oneself," the monologist remains in bed, suffering with a fever, when his visitor comes to see him. Thus, it is not surprising that some critics, notably Emile Henriot, have described Clamence as "taking masochistic pleasure in degrading himself," and his confession as "cynical and vain," even "disgusting." Instead, it would appear that this undertaking of "self-degradation" singularly yields him up to torture and that his cynicism is rooted in an emotion of pathos that is all the more painful for remaining suppressed. As for his irony, it is the hair shirt of his clear-sightedness; the more he presses against it, the more it galls him. And does one not, as well, touch a form of tragedy with this conscious confronting of evil discovered within the self, humiliated in its pure revolt by the ineluctable infirmity of its nature? For it must be specified—yet is it really necessary?—that this Camusian hero is of the line of Sisyphus and cannot conceive of appealing to divine aid, having "no religion whatever," no least feeling of transcendency.

The solution of the judge-penitent has therefore not offered a solution to anything at all.[64] Clamence is aware of this, but "when you don't like your life, when you know that you must change it, you don't have a choice, do you?" The fury of impotence then assumes the mask of triumph. One proclaims one's happiness: ". . . I'm happy, I'm happy, I tell you. I forbid you not to believe that I'm happy. I'm dying of happiness!" (p. 166) The anxious insistence does not, alas, convince us, but rather the contrary.

[64] *Le Mythe de Sisyphe* suggested only one way of living the absurd destiny: to make every effort "to maintain before one's eyes that sentiment of the absurd revealed by the consciousness." We find an attitude very close to this in Clamence, who comes full circle in his revolt against evil by maintaining himself in evil.

A few seconds later, recovered from the excitation which had determined him to arm himself with ostentatious glory, exhausted by that access of fever, the "empty prophet for mediocre times" comes to grips with himself and with the inferno of reality: "I'm afraid I let myself go; but I'm not crying. We let ourselves go at times, we doubt the evidence, even when we've discovered the secrets of a good life. My solution, of course, is not the ideal." The truth appears, and with it the wound opens: "How to become another person? Impossible. What one must be is nobody, one must forget oneself for someone, at least once. But how?" (pp. 166-167)

There is no solution to the problem; the shadows of guilt are dense and invincible; the fall, irremediable. Clamence has disguised as a makeshift a defeat from which he will never recover. All the same, this does not give us the right to repulse the mirror he holds out to us, nor to flee from the light that he has projected on "the sadness of the common condition of man and the despair of not being able to escape it." And here is where the moralist lies in wait for us.

A *disturbing myth.* Springing from a personal experience, Camus' narrative work is stripped to the bare bones of myth, the myth *sub specie aeternitatis.* This quite classic preoccupation with universality is here expressed in the intentions of the protagonist: "I mingle what concerns me with what concerns others. I take our common features and the experiences we have endured together, the weaknesses that we share, the good behavior, the man of the time, in short, as he exists in me and in others. With that material I fabricate a portrait which is a portrait of everyone and no one." (p. 161)

Thus, the judge-penitent's confession implicates our own even before asking for it. His clear gaze penetrates us and forces us to assume his cruel discoveries with him. And which one of us will not admit recognizing himself in this figure of an upright man, but a man who has never had enough sincerity and courage to denounce openly his moral comfort and beneath the very appearance of virtue to denounce the omnipotence of his egoism? Come what may, we must concede that we are all accomplices.

After the optimism of *La Peste*, the impossible revolt of Clamence and his fallen-angel's acrimony seem to mark a *volte-face* of Camus' attitude which rather sharply drives his thought back towards the negative position of *L'Etranger*. Just as man's need of enlightenment and justice will make him come to grief against the absurd walls, so his demands for purity and his yearning for innocence will painfully exhaust him in his effort to surmount the fatal inevitability of his faults. The teaching is new and is superimposed upon the other; but there is the same refusal to be resigned, the same certitude void of hope, the same imprisonment.

La Chute no more annuls the truths of *La Peste*, than *La Peste* annuled the truths of *L'Etranger*. What human dignity can accomplish against historical and collective evil is one thing, what remains for human dignity to accomplish against the evil of the individual conscience is another thing.[65]

After Meursault (in *L'Etranger*), after Maria (in *Le Malentendu*), after *Caligula,* Jean-Baptiste Clamence presents a new extreme case, and the narrative of his experience aims less at instructing than at disturbing us. His rejection of all complacency, all subterfuge, all compromise overwhelms us with revelations that are at times intolerable, but such intransigency, through the absolute purity to which it refers, heals and stimulates us in the long run, and far from casting us down into despair, whips up our energy to live a life finally disintoxicated and freed from the imposture of false satisfactions. The clairvoyance which the poet already

[65] The question aired in our note 39 here finds a clearer and, in a way, a more categorical answer.

magnified in *Noces* remains for strong souls the only possible revenge against the rigors of fate.

An undertaking of "moderate demoralization,"[66] *La Chute* contents itself with repeating "to consciences that they are not without blemishes,"[67] and this reminder, after the warnings of *L'Homme Révolté*, finally raises to prominence a preoccupation which up to this point had only insinuated itself discreetly into the main theme of revolt. One should recall the anxious soul searchings of Tarrou (in *La Peste*), and the scruples of the young revolutionaries in *Les Justes*. Kaliayev, confronting the Grand Duchess who urges him to repent, exclaims, "Let me prepare to die. If I do not die, then I shall be a murderer"; Clamence, evoking the torment of Jesus, involuntarily responsible for the massacre of the innocents, slips in a little remark that is not without some connection with his own obsession: "Oh! Who would have believed that the crime is not so much in causing death as in not dying oneself!" (p. 131) These quotations placed side by side illuminate the characters, showing their consanguinity, and attest once more to the intimate solidarity that reigns among works apparently foreign to each other.

[66] and [67] Unpublished statements by Camus, quoted by R. Quillot, *op. cit.*, p. 238.

L'Exil et Le Royaume[68]

This collection of six short stories, in which *La Chute* was originally destined to be included, confirms the mastery of Camus and reveals in this stylist possibilities of renewal which, far from obliterating his personal and inimitable stamp, heighten it with unexpected charm. Never have we been given the opportunity to have a more exact view of his art than in these pages where the appropriateness of the style to the subject matter is completely realized six times in succession. Nor have we ever been better able to perceive the exact physiognomy and the orientation of his past work than in the new perspective opened up by this series of narratives.

The reason is that here the narration develops according to the very laws and rhythm of the literary form, evolving in descriptive passages of imagery, lingering over a psychological shudder, carefully recounting the action in detail, capturing the gesture and fixing the attitude; here reality irrupts, charged with sensations, complexity of movement, opulence; a veritable flowering.

And it is not merely a question of an aesthetic, of a certain way of gathering and "filtering" reality; the

[68] Gallimard, Paris, 1957.

ethical point of view asserts itself equally in the effort to comprehend total life, to seize the diversity and the poignancies of life.

In the allegorical form of his previous works, the linear curve of the narrative not only was drawn with an extreme economy of detail, but it also set out only to describe an extreme behavior, and to extract from it only one single verity of living experience. Unity being always a preoccupation of Camus, he sought, in the past, to compensate for its apparent betrayal by making one work respond to another: *L'Etranger* answered by *La Peste*, *La Peste* answered by *La Chute*.

But *L'Exil et le Royaume* "contrasts an attempt at plenitude with the achievements of abstraction," notes Gaëtan Picon, who, clearly perceiving this new phase, concludes thus: "The book invites us to seize the very pulsation of existence, opening and closing, revealing and concealing itself, increasing and decreasing. To the moralist who isolates and parcels out, there seems to have succeeded, here, a poet who assembles and restores the unique throbbing of life."[69]

Nevertheless, these simple tales, situations arrested and held as if suspended, carry a certain power of abstraction, since all of them—and each in its own way

[69] "À propos de *L'Exil et Le Royaume*," in *Le Mercure de France*, May, 1957.

—illustrate the same theme, thus giving unity to this collection, beneath the diversity of expression.

North Africa, the land from which Camus has constantly drawn his best inspiration, forms the setting of the first four tales; the fifth one would seem to exploit his experiences in Paris, and the last one draws upon memories of a voyage to South America in the summer of 1949. Even so, these various settings impose no geographical necessity; they merely provide the atmosphere, magical at times, for the inner drama of the characters.

The first story, *La Femme Adultère*, places on stage a sensitive and imaginative woman, who has been dragged along on a business trip among the villages of the high plateau of southern Algeria by her preoccupied husband. Confronting there the silent Arabs, particularly that soldier with the aspect of a jackal who "surveyed her with his light eyes" in the arid and glacial loneliness of the desert, she discovers at once her solitude and her servitude, and all the things her cheated heart has confusedly yearned for—and, till now, been denied. Perceiving an encampment of nomads in the distance, she begins to feel a warm and irresistible complicity with those few men "who wandered without respite, who possessed nothing, but who served no one, miserable yet free lords of a strange realm." "She knew only that this realm had been promised her from the beginning of time but that never would it be hers, unless at this fugitive instant, perhaps, when she opened her eyes upon the sky suddenly immobile and upon the floods of motionless light, while the sound of voices that drifted up from the Arab village became, all at once, hushed."

A few hours later, she leaves the hotel to flee into the night and to yield herself, rapturously, to the possession of the "sky in movement." She then returns to her room, to the marriage bed, to mediocrity, to her exile, and begins to weep "with all her tears, unable to hold them back."

It is a short story that fills all the strict requirements of the form: against a realistic background the author outlines for us, as with the light touches of the engraver's needle, a dry-point which depicts all the delicate shadings of a mood experienced in a moment of time.

In *Le Renégat ou un Esprit confus* ("The Renegade or a Mind Confused"), we are caught in a situation of horror and atrocity. The story is told in a nightmarish monologue delivered by a man who has had his tongue torn out. The tale is of a young missionary with a peasant background, a stubborn, hard-headed, impulsive individual—product of a childhood on the high plateau of the Massif Central in France, with a "coarse" father and a "brute" of a mother—who is so enraptured with proselytism that he mistakes his fierce will to power (disguised by an inclination for martyrdom) for charity. Despite the advice and warnings of his superiors, he had wanted to visit "the town of salt . . . at the frontier of the lands occupied by the whites and the blacks" and convert the barbarous tribes to his religion. He was not afraid of physical harm; on the contrary, he courted injuries: ". . . by the way in which I will endure them, I will subjugate the savages, like a powerful sun. Powerful, yes, that was the word I constantly rolled on my tongue, I dreamed of absolute power, the power before which people fall to their knees, the power that forces the adversary to capitulate and which, in short, converts the adversary . . ."

Tortures are, indeed, reserved for him, and without stint, but no one bends the knee. And he it was who, after long torment and the mutilation inflicted upon him, began to deny his faith and recognize and worship, as evil incarnate, the fetich that was in the house where he was imprisoned.

He had been fooled: good was a chimera; "only the reign of wickedness was without flaw." The slave and admirer of his tormentors, he conceives of but one way to obtain freedom: to become cruel like them, closed to pity, ferocious, bloodthirsty.

So it is that when he learns, one day, that an army

chaplain, riding ahead of a garrison of twenty men, has been authorized to penetrate the village to look after the children there, he flies into a feverish rage of hatred. More ingenious in wickedness than he could ever be for his own good, he manages to escape and, armed with an old rifle he has seized, stations himself beside the road. When his co-religionist arrives, he fires upon "his impotence and charity, fires upon everything that delays the advent of Evil." Crucified by his masters, who fear reprisals, forsaken by his fetich as he had been by his God, he is filled with anguished doubt: "Oh! Have I been fooled again!" In the moment of anguish there is revealed to him the earthly realm which he has always ignored, and he cannot keep back this overwhelming entreaty: "O men in other times fraternal, sole recourse, O solitude, do not forsake me!"

Rejected by love from his tender infancy, seminarist impatient for revenge, priest of pride and of absolute power, votary of hate, victim and torturer, this "intelligent mule" has experienced to the end the calvary of his infatuation; only the pangs of death have been able to make him understand that the only possible way out for the exile is to be found between rejection of servitude and resignation of power.

Les Muets ("The Mute Men") are workingmen in a small coopering shop. Defeated in a strike, they return to their jobs, having formed a coalition of silence against their employer who tries in vain to break it down and secure their good will and sympathy. Assuredly, they have it in for him; yet he would have liked nothing better than to satisfy their demands. But let misfortune crash down upon that man whom they have excluded from their fraternal universe, and they are immediately at a loss, "with their rough hands hanging down uselessly against their old sawdust-covered pants . . ." But not one word will be pronounced, and not one gesture even vaguely made.

Shut off from each other in their different social categories, all these individuals suffer at being exiled from the realm in which love and understanding, without reserve, could finally exist.

I do not know if *L'Hôte* ("The Guest") has more right to our admiration than the other stories, but its simplicity of plot and the bitter-sweet poesy which it distills confer a beauty and, yes, a soundness upon it which has a disintoxicating effect.

The scene is a high Algerian plateau, to which winter has suddenly come in a blizzard, isolating a schoolhouse that clings to the side of a hill and is now deserted by its pupils. In this school, assaulted by the wind, there is a solitary man, the schoolmaster, fortunately with enough provisions to "sustain a siege." "The country was like that, a cruel place to live, even without the presence of men who, however, did nothing to improve matters. But Daru was born there, and he felt exiled everywhere else."

And now two men climb up the hill to his refuge: a gendarme with an Arab at the end of a rope .The Arab has killed a cousin in a quarrel over grain. He will have to be taken to a place twenty kilometers away. But since the gendarme is obliged to return immediately to his village, the order is given for the schoolmaster to substitute for him on this errand.

Daru refuses: "The stupid crime committed by that man revolted him, but to hand him over to the authorities was against his principles." He signs a paper attesting to the fact that the prisoner has been left in his charge, and the gendarme goes away.

Next morning, after an hour's walk, the schoolmaster puts a parcel of food and some money into the Arab's hands; then, turning him away from the road to the east which ends at "government and the police," he shows the Arab the road towards the south, where are pastures and nomads and where he could find a refuge —the road to liberty.

His stupefaction knows no bounds when, after a few minutes, he perceives the Arab "who was slowly walking along the road to the prison."

Back in his classroom, the schoolmaster reads the following inscription on the blackboard, "traced with chalk by an awkward hand: 'You have handed over our brother. You will pay for it.'"

And this threat of an invisible witness, in which once more may be read the "misunderstanding," makes him touch the bottom of his solitude and feel the immanence, in the midst of his realm, of an inevitable exile. Without being either the slave or the master of anyone, and to safeguard the liberty of that innocence, he had offended his old friend, the gendarme; the Arab had chosen punishment, and he himself will be exposed, on the morrow, to unjustifiable reprisals . . .

Because of its plan, its symbolical plot-lines, and the humor which constantly underlines it, the narrative entitled *Jonas* smacks essentially of the philosophical tale. The protagonist may be summed up by a few characteristics: naiveté, simplicity, light-heartedness and light-mindedness, stupid optimism; the action, in brief, is a sequence of events which fade into each other in a smooth continuity.

Jonas is a happy man. He has left his family's business —a publishing house—to follow his vocation as an artist. He has married the woman of his dreams, who has given him, in quick succession, three adorable children. He has a sure friend, and fortune has favored him—

he is famous, his paintings sell, the newspapers speak of him in terms of praise, his name fills the important art chronicles.

But Jonas' head is not turned by success; he believes in his guiding star and attributes this sequence of good fortune to it.

Alas, reputation has its drawbacks. He is invited everywhere, his help is demanded everywhere and in all sorts of ways, his correspondence monopolizes his time more and more, his home is more and more invaded by people who are full of respect for him but not for his work, and his work suffers. His family also begins to be in the way: the children are growing up and the apartment lacks space.

But Jonas is good, generous, responsive. Around him he sees only solicitude, affability, kindness. How to withhold himself from the presence of all these people, even though they are troublesome? And then, too, there's his star, to whose keeping he entrusts himself blindly.

Poor man, he had not foreseen that his star might grow dim! The day comes when the critics are more reticent than usual; next day, more severe; the day after, aggressive, ferocious. If one were to believe them, Jonas is finished as an artist.

And in fact his inspiration seems to be in some difficulty. He does not manage to work as before. To find a semblance of solitude, Jonas leaves his studio for the bedroom: the visitors, though more infrequent, follow him there. Then he installs himself in the corridor; after that, he shifts to the shower-room, and finally he ends up in the kitchen. What is he now painting? Nothing, now. He tries hard, but in vain.

Then, on various pretexts, he begins going out. He discovers that alcohol fleetingly illumines a creative fire within him, similar to that of his days of feverish creativity. He even goes so far as to succumb to the "friendship" of a few women. Despair of the betrayed wife, tears, repentance of the culprit.

Jonas takes hold of himself. He wants to paint, he will force himself to paint. He needs to find the light of his guiding star again. Absolute solitude is indispensable. What will he do? He builds a kind of garret cubbyhole in the right angle formed by the two corridors of his apartment. There, at least, "he will disturb no one." Ingenious and aimiable Jonas!

Shut into his bird-roost which he ends up by never leaving at all, the artist reflects. "He had to pin down finally that secret which was not merely the secret of art, he saw quite well. That is why he did not light the lamp." And that secret would be discovered shortly afterwards when, exhausted and at the end of his strength, he fell down and his canvas, which had remained entirely blank, was taken from him. In the centre of it a word was written in very small letters, "a word that one could decipher, but without knowing whether it should be read as *solitary* or *solidarity*."

A play on words which is not merely gratuitous, but is charged with profound value, since it synthesizes the meaning of the symbol. Solitary, yes, that is the condition of the realm of the creator who must in no way be distracted from his effort; but at the same time he must endure banishment from the human community. Solidarity, yes, since the artist is a man, that "social animal," who has his affections and weaknesses, his need for communication; but then, his vocation, deranged, becomes unresponsive, his genius dwindles: "Everything won for life is lost for art." (Oscar Wilde)

It would seem that *La Pierre qui Pousse* was reserved, for more than one reason, to end the collection of stories. By far the most important, with *Jonas*, this story is also one in which the author demonstrates most completely his resources as a writer of prose. And also, its conclusion displays, brighter than the flashes of light glimpsed up to this point, Camus' optimism in its full brightness.

True, some portions such as the evocation of the Brazilian forest, with which the narrative opens, or the extremely exact descriptions of a *macumba* and of a religious procession, while heightening the feeling of the truth of the tale by the authenticity of the local color, give no less the impression of splendid adornments.[70] One feels that the author lingers over these portions as if with pleasure, ensnared by his own spells. Reality, here, takes its revenge.

D'Arrast, an engineer, fleeing Europe, has been in Brazil for a month. The notables of the small town of Iguapa have engaged him to construct a dike "which will prevent the periodical flooding of the waterfront sections." In reality, D'Arrast, like Tarrou and Clamence, is trying to escape an oppressive memory; "Someone was going to die on my account . . ." A more imperious necessity than his profession, then, has required this expatriation. He waited, in the red heat of the humid days, under the tiny stars of night, despite the tasks that were his, the dikes to build, the roads to open, as if the work he had come to do here was but a pretext, the occasion of a surprise, or of an encounter that he did not even imagine, but which would wait patiently for him to the end of time."

He is far from suspecting that the native with whom he has engaged in conversation will be the instrument of that encounter. Ship's cook on an oil tanker which

[70] All the elements of "the dance in honor of St. George" (pages 210 *et seq.*) had already figured in *Une macumba au Brésil* (extract of a travel diary), published in *Livres de France*, Hachette, Paris, November 1951, pp. 5-7.

caught fire one night, the man had gone down with the lifeboat cast out to sea and was very near drowning when, sighting in the distance the dome of the Iguapa church, he had promised Jesus that, if saved, he would walk to the church in a religious procession, carrying a stone weighing a hundred pounds on his head. Jesus had saved him; he must keep his promise, and that, not later than the following day.

But that evening and all night long there will be a *macumba* in the long-house, it is the festival "for Saint George." The ship's cook knows the irresistible spell exercised over him by this part-Christian, part-pagan ceremony, in which the celebrant dances and sings until he falls into a trance, to facilitate the descent of God into him. "And then, there are the cigars and the saints and the women. You forget everything, you don't obey any more." Yet he must save his strength for the carrying of the stone . . . He asks D'Arrast to accompany him. "Come to the dance. Afterwards, you can take me away. If you don't, I'll stay and I'll dance, I'll not be able, perhaps, to keep myself from it . . ."

D'Arrast accepts. The cook dances all night long, although the engineer reminds him of his promise. Next morning, his strength fails him; the stone slips to the ground and, exhausted, he collapses.

Then, D'Arrast took up the burden, walking to the

church square, after which, "not knowing why," he struck off in the direction of the water front, reached the cook's hovel, entered it and, "with one single movement, he threw the stone upon the fire that was still burning red in the middle of the room." The vow was accomplished. From then on, the foreigner would be a part of the home he had saved from disgrace.

For D'Arrast, it was life "beginning again."

Exiled from a Europe "of shame and wrath, exiled among these languid and restless fools who dance to die," exiled from himself, he had, by associating himself with the pious beliefs of one of his fellow men, reconquered his realm, his faith in an earthly fraternity untrammeled by History and attuned to his "pitiful and terrible love."

Part iii.

THE AESTHETICIAN
AND ARTIST

iii.

THE AESTHETICIAN
AND ARTIST

It is not surprising that Camus has extended his thinking to questions of literary creation and to the problems
of his own aesthetic, nor that he has applied to this
endeavor the same lucidity that led him from the absurdist to the rebellious position. He sees man-as-man
and man-as-artist as an entity; everything that concerns
the one implicates the other. Conscious of the dignity
of his mission, he could not stop halfway and leave the
demands of his vocation beyond the conquests of his
thought. Thus we find that each of the two phases of
his moral reflection comports its aesthetic corollary. *Le
Mythe de Sisyphe* devotes its entire third section to
"Absurd Creation" *(création absurde); L'Homme Révolté*
returns to the question in its fourth chapter, under the
heading "Rebellion and Art" *(création révoltée).*

1. ABSURD CREATION

It is defined as being the expression of an "illumination" by which the conscious mind brutally discovers the nonsense of the universe and the meaninglessness of human life. The clairvoyant artist is thereby offered the chance of alerting his awareness and of directing its adventures, since in the course of creative effort the artist forces himself to remain mentally "detached" from life, keeping the perspective which will enable him to apply his images exactly "to what is reasonless," while bewaring of letting anything of this effort appear or of introducing into his work an order, organization, or significance of which his model is utterly devoid. Admiration has been expressed for the way this candid technique was employed in *L'Etranger*, which is a veritable decalcomania, an exact reproduction, a "miming" of the absurd; here the creative attitude expresses itself in revolt, freedom, and diversity with the same poignant limpidity brought by the author to the elaboration of his line of thought.

The work of art can no more admit a meaning than the life whose mechanical unfolding it seeks to reflect. The work of art explains nothing and screens from the reader even the least indication of that consciousness affronting a sentient world which repudiates it. In its gratuitousness, it is careful not to entertain the least principle of explanation, the most furtive illusion, the faintest glimmer of hope. For its creator, it forever represents but a useless thing. "Art can never be so well served as by a negative thought . . . To work and create 'for nothing,' to model in clay, to know that one's creation has no future . . ." (*Le Mythe de Sisyphe*, p. 154)

The freedom of the creation which nothing solicits, neither thesis nor doctrine, and which consequently has complete access to the field of reality, brings about the diversity of its realizations. One after another, the works will succeed each other, without any apparent bond to unite them; but from the whole body of the work the thought will radiate like the fire of a many-faceted diamond. Thought, for Camus, is the opposite of ideas. It is the mirror of the world and not the augmenting of the world by adding to it an original point of view.

The artist finds in his work no consolation, no reason for hope, no outlet which will enable him to escape the "absurd walls" and give a meaning to his life. His creation represents nothing to him but a means of strengthening his absurdist attitude and sharpening his vigilance; it is a veritable *ascesis* which "requires daily effort, self-discipline, and exact appreciation of the bounds of truth, moderation, and strength." Understandably, one can claim that it is "the overwhelming evidence of man's sole dignity; the stubborn revolt against his condition, the perseverance in an effort considered sterile." (*Le Mythe de Sisyphe,* p. 156)

2. REBELLION AND ART

The absurdist work of art is neither more nor less free of contradiction than is the attitude upon which it is based. By the simple fact of existing, it at least signifies the nonsignificance of the world and of life. In art as in ethics, the absurd must, then, be surpassed. By the notion of revolt introduced into his philosophical meditation, the author makes his aesthetic thought accomplish a progress which we have already traced from *L'Etranger* to *La Peste.*

All the arts, when one comes to think of it, obey one unique impetus: they reject the world and at the same time consent to it. The composer of music takes sounds offered in their formless and scattered state and "extracts from the natural disorder a unity satisfying to the mind and heart." Sculpture stylizes the attitude of the model and, without refusing to give resemblance, seeks to free it from anecdote in such a way as to express "the gesture, the attitude, or the empty stare which will sum up all the gestures and all the stares in the world." The land-

scape painter or the painter of still-lifes chooses his subject in time and space, isolates within the limitations of
a canvas and in an unchangeable light a selection of
scattered realities situated in an infinite mobility of
light. As for subject-painting, it fixes in one single choice
and isolation the image of human actions which, in
fact, appear detached from their destiny and "continue
to live, while ceasing to be mortal."

The author now devotes himself to an analysis of the
novel, and notes that fiction, remarkably enough, coin-
cides historically with the beginning of the spirit of
revolt. By common consent the novel is expected to open
up an imaginary world to the reader, into which he
escapes and takes refuge from the crushing world of
reality. More than one revolutionary reformer has taken
up this argument—using it as a red herring, actually—
to justify condemnation of creative art. However, it is
quite clear that the majority of men, although they may
reject reality, do not for that reason want to withhold
themselves from it or escape from it. On the contrary,
they suffer from the fact that reality, forever uncom-
pleted, forever eludes them. They are devoured with a
longing to discover the complete curve of their existence,
to "know where it leads, to dominate the course of the
flood, in a word, to seize life as destiny." They experience
the heartbreak of wanting their love to endure, while

knowing that it will not endure, of wanting to possess the loved one without ever being able utterly to possess, to burn with the feeling of the absolute and to learn that "absolute communion throughout a lifetime is an impossible demand." Finally, they would like to assemble and coordinate their existence, give it the unity it lacks, organize their ideas and actions in such a way as to give their life a unity of style.

The world of the novel exactly responds to all these aspirations. "It is only a rectification of the world we live in, according to our deepest wishes." The same world as our own, however, the same sentiments and language; with one sole difference, one single superiority: in the novel the heroes pursue their destiny to the end, their passions are engraved upon it in firm and continuous lines, everything is resolved in a pure, clear, and perfect curve.

Thus, in offering to man's metaphysical aspirations the opportunity of surmounting for a moment his impotence and the possibility of serene appeasement, the novel reveals itself as a movement of revolt against creation, which it is pleased to rectify. The novel protests against the imperfection of a real world, in which nothing lasts or is completed, by insisting on an imaginary world "in which suffering can, if it likes, endure till death, where passions are never bemused, where people are given over to obsessions and are always present to one another." (*L'Homme Révolté*, p. 326)

In order to make us grasp concretely this unity to which the fictional work aspires, Camus studies and compares two opposite attempts: the American novel of the 1930s and 1940s, and the work of Marcel Proust. The American novel depicts humanity objectively, without commentaries, strictly abstaining from accounting for the motives or the deep springs of behavior. Enchained by their daily automatisms, the characters perform before our eyes like so many puppets assimilated to the same significance and "interchangeable." The sought-for unity seems to be reached, but it is a unity of stage-lighting, not of structure, it is "a degraded unity." Instead of trying to obtain unity by the process of revolt, the authors of the "tough" novels have found it more expeditious to deny what diversifies and individualizes human reality: the inner life. The imaginary man thus described represents nothing but an abstract and imaginary being; the "correction" of reality undertaken here amounts to an amputation.

Quite the contrary, Marcel Proust rejects reality but does not deny it. His world is the world of the inner life, of memory, in which he chooses to resuscitate from a present moment such and such a fragment of the past and at the same time to discard "immense blank spaces" from life. He surmounts the dispersal of the actual world by bringing together "into a superior form of unity, the memory of the past and the immediate sensation, the sprained foot and the happy days of times gone by." *Le Temps retrouvé* ("Time Regained") is creation without God; in it, Proust consecrates in an eternity of perfection the victory of his unified universe and the victory of man over "the powers of death and oblivion."

We now understand that, on the aesthetic as on the historical level, the movement of true revolt asserts itself in the equilibrium of a Yes or a No. If absolute negation, the work of art escapes into a purely formal creation, from which "reality is completely expelled." If absolute affirmation, it sinks to the level of "brute reality." Despite their color, the *"roman rose"* or the *"roman noir"* are twin brothers and the offspring of the same nihilism. The unity obtained in both cases by the suppression of one of the terms of revolt (reality or consciousness) is revealed to be quite illusory. The most strictly formalistic art, even the most geometrical, cannot dispense utterly with reality; the most realistic art, even photographic art, cannot help but interpret and betray—no matter how slightly—the sentient world. "On the other hand, unity in art appears at the limit of the transformation that the artist imposes on reality

... This rectification of reality which the artist undertakes by his language and by a redistribution of elements derived from reality is called style and gives the recreated universe its unity and its boundaries." (*L'Homme Révolté* p. 332) In the work inspired by revolt, the style will consequently bear witness to an uninterrupted tension between form and matter, between a faithfulness to reality and a conscious protestation against certain aspects of it.[71] The style will be just sufficiently present to take on the image of the world as far as the form towards which it tends, but will nonetheless attempt to efface its presence "so that the demand which gives birth to art should be expressed in its most extreme tension." (*L'Homme Révolté*, p. 335)

3. THE MISSION OF THE ARTIST

On this point, too, Albert Camus has clearly explained himself several times. First of all, in an address made at

[71] Actually the same concept, although not centred upon the notion of revolt, is expressed by Wladimir Weidlé in *Les Abeilles d'Aristée*, Essai sur de destin actuel des Lettres et des Arts, (Gallimard, 1954): "It is impossible to dream of installing man in the written work, so long as he has not been imagined in his totality. Otherwise, under the name of 'man,' the writer ends up with the sub-human and forgets that empty form is exactly equivalent to raw material, incapable of assuming a form. No choice is possible between a purely artificial literature and a literature which repudiates all art under the pretext of seeing nothing in it but artifice. Man dispossessed of art is as inhuman as art deprived of man. For the measure of man, his grandeur as well as his misery, is art."

the Salle Pleyel in November 1948 and published under
the title *"Les Témoins de la Liberté"* in *Actuelles I* (pp.
251-267). What should the attitude of a writer be at
a time "when Cain kills Abel in the name of logic and
afterwards asks to be rewarded by the Legion of
Honor?" Can the world of art adjust itself to the ideological world, can the ambition of the artist adjust itself
to that of the conqueror? True, the one and the other
meet in their desire to overcome the disorders of reality,
but the very movement of their revolt places them ir-
remediably in opposition. The first seeks unity "in the
harmony of opposites," the second "in totality, which
is the wiping out of differences." The work of art builds
its living unity in argument, in comprehension, and in
love; imperialism installs its mute empire of slavery in
blood and hatred. All artists worthy of the name reject
such an empire. By their vocation they are "the witnesses of the flesh, not of the law," the witnesses of
freedom. They are the ones upon whom it is incumbent
to proclaim to the face of the world, and before the
spectacle of its totalitarian folly, that "it is worth more
to be wrong without killing anyone and in allowing
others to talk, than to be right in the midst of silence
and charnel-houses." (*Actuelles* I, p. 267)

In fact, the artist does not *choose* to fight against
tyranny, and it is beside the point to talk about "en-

gagement." Simply, fidelity to his vocation does not
allow him to remain silent before the tyrant who vocif-
erates, nor to abstain from exalting life, when history
is preparing to swallow up humanity in the abyss of
nothingness. This is what the author reminds us of in the
chapter "The Artist and his Time," which groups, in
Actuelles II (pp. 173-182), a series of replies to some
questions asked on the radio or in foreign newspapers.
"The miner who is exploited or who is shot down, the
slaves of the concentration camps and the slaves of the
colonies, the persecuted legions throughout the world
have need, for their part, that all those who can speak
should give voice to their silence and not hold
themselves apart from them." At any rate there can be
no question, when one has placed his life at the service
of beauty, of his apostasy in behalf of no matter what
"social preachings." In this hour when the world seems
to have gone beyond nihilism, it has as much need of
beauty as of love, and it is inconceivable that it could
do without one of these values without necessarily having to abdicate the other. Between the ivory tower and
the roll call of "the social church," is there room for a
creative attitude which will reconcile aesthetic demands
with the duty of brotherhood? Yes, on condition that
we endure the tension of the man who imposes his social
will upon himself as artist and his aesthetic scruples as

artist upon his will as man. The creative artist from that point onward must accept the dangers which threaten him and repel the bitterness his sense of alienation sometimes inspires. Let him never lose sight of the fact that "all authentic creation is a gift to the future."

This brings us to the conclusion reached in *L'Homme Révolté* (pp. 341-342) about this apocalyptic light that art renders to the road of revolution: "In upholding beauty, we prepare the way for the day of regeneration when civilization will give first place—far above the formal principles and degraded values of history—to this living virtue on which is founded the common dignity of man and the world in which he lives."

4. THE END OF ART

Camus has had the chance to air these convictions in public, notably in a talk that he gave at Turin on November 26, 1954 and, during the following days, successively at Genoa, Milan, and Rome. He reaffirmed them in a recent interview with Jean Bloch-Michel, and underscored the strikingly delicate position of the contemporary artist who is faced with a choice between total engagement or total isolation: "That's how it is with the artist of our age: he runs the risk, if he stays in his ivory tower, of cutting himself off from reality, or, if he gallops forever around the political arena, of drying up. The ticklish paths of true art lie somewhere between the two. It seems to me that the writer should not ignore the conflicts of his time, and that he should take part in them when he knows that he can. But he should also keep, or from time to time recover, a definite perspective towards our history. Every work presupposes some factual content to which a creator has given shape. Though the artist should share in the misfortunes of his age, he must also try to stand off a bit to contemplate and formalize what he sees. This eternal return, this tension which can be, frankly, a dangerous game at times, is the burden of the artist today. Perhaps this means that, in short order, there will no longer be any artists. But maybe not. It is a question of time, of energy, of freedom, and also of chance."

When Camus speaks here of a work so balanced between a negation and an affirmation, of the work of a witness (not of a partisan), and of a work of art (not of dilettantism), he is assuming that literature has a moral purpose. But it would be totally false to confuse what he says with a mere moralistic pretension. He is very clear about this: ". . . I detest virtue that is only smugness, I detest the frightful morality of the world, and I detest it because it ends, just like absolute cynicism, in demoralizing men and keeping them from running their own lives with their own just measures of meanness and magnificence."

Triumphing at once in the exigency of reality and in the expendability of illusion, the work of art charges every consciousness with the vibrations of the same freedom that has set it in motion: "The end of art, the end of each life, can only be to add to the sum of freedom and responsibility that is in every heart and in the world. It can never be, whatever the provocation, to diminish or to suppress, even provisionally, this freedom. There are works that try to sway men and to convert them to authoritarian rules. Others cater to what is bad in men, to their fears and their hates. I find no value in such works. No master work has ever been based on hatred or contempt. On the contrary, there has never been a work of true art that has not in the end added to the personal freedom of everyone who has known and loved it."

5. THE NOBEL PRIZE FOR LITERATURE, 1957

The ultimate confirmation of Camus' literary theory and practice came on Thursday, October 17, 1957, when the Swedish Academy awarded him the Nobel Prize for Literature and congratulated the laureate "for his important literary work which illuminates, with penetrating purposiveness, the problems of the human conscience in the contemporary world." The award was all the greater a distinction because of the achievements of Camus' competitors, prominent among whom were André Malraux, Saint-John Perse, and Nikos Kazantzakis.

Camus was surprised by the news of his success:

"Had I been a judge, I would have voted for André Malraux," he said.

This tribute—which is not mere courtesy—is typical of what the man is and always has been: sincere, genuine, uninhibited, completely indifferent to his fame, and, to borrow a phrase from his friend, René Char, "a stranger to himself."

When all is said, the award of the Academy at Stockholm merely heightens the brilliance of Camus' well-founded fame. It confirms, in effect, only that he has arrived: at 43 years of age, in the full flower of his creative genius, Albert Camus still awaits his future, secure in the harvest that he has already reaped.

199

Appendix

REFLEXIONS SUR
LA GUILLOTINE

Réflexions sur la Guillotine, which Albert Camus published last May in a tandem edition with Arthur Koestler's *Réflexions sur la Potence,*[72] has been read with such interest both in France and abroad that it seems fitting to give the work some special notice over and above the mention it received in the original plan of this book. Actually, *Réflexions sur la Guillotine* first appeared in two successive editions of *La Nouvelle N.R.F.* (Nos. 54 and 55, June and July, 1957). As articles on a seemingly new and topical subject, they have been classed with the "Rediscoveries" of the author. Such a classification is misleading, for they are really restatements, with greater precision and subtler technique, of sentiments that he has avowed with greater or lesser insistence throughout his career. Did not *The Stranger,* for example, constitute a brief against capital punishment? Since then, the author has been persistently haunted by the horror

[72] Arthur Koestler-Albert Camus, *Réflexions sur la Peine Capitale,* with an Introduction and Appraisal by Jean Bloch-Michel, Paris, Calmann-Levy, 1957.

of legal execution and, in a larger sense, of rationalized murder. Is it not possible to cite the confession of the character Tarrou in *The Plague,* the indecision and heartache of Kaliayev, the assassin in *Les Justes,* and the disturbing insights of the judge-penitent in *The Fall?* Is it necessary to evoke the bruising pages of *The Rebel?* Albert Camus was, as it were, ordained to plead before the French people the case for the abolition of capital punishment that Koestler had successfully presented, in 1955, to his English public.

Before beginning his argument, the author analyzes the nature of his conviction: "Across the years, I have found the idea of the death sentence either too painful to think about or such a sleazy rationalization that it has outraged my sense of logic. However, I was willing to suppose that I was being swayed by my imagination. But, truthfully, I have come across nothing in these past weeks that has weakened my conviction or forced me to alter my argument. In fact, I have discovered other arguments to support those I originally held. Now I subscribe wholly to Koestler's contention: capital punishment is a disgrace to our society and its advocates cannot reasonably defend their position." (pp. 128-129)

It would be worthwhile to give here a brief synopsis of Camus' arguments before going on to show how they relate to his characteristic ideas:

a) *The assumption of the modern State that capital punishment is an exemplary sentence which seeks to deter rather than to punish crime is shameful and ambiguous.*

If the State actually subscribes to this principle, then it should give executions the widest publicity. Instead, it carries them out in secret and even takes pains to conceal the objective reports of the witnesses and the doctors who have written about the procedure. The evolution of public sensibility has forced the State to take measures that refute the traditional defense of capital punishment.

b) *Capital punishment does not prevent crime, and it even arouses an unfortunate morbidity in certain minds.*

Surely it does not intimidate the majority who are apt to be the hapless victims of the crime. But it also does nothing to deter those who make their living by crime. The mere threat of legal vengeance cannot check intense passion, and the fear of death seizes the murderer after his conviction, not before his crime. The instinct for self-preservation is too unstable—it is even at times completely supplanted by its opposite, the will to self-destruction—to be paralyzed by the fear of death which, if the legislator is to be believed, should be a sufficient deterrent in itself. Finally, far from accomplishing its desired end, the spectacle of an execution sometimes succeeds in arousing latent traces of sadism in the public mind and in winning a hideous fame for certain criminals.

c) *Capital punishment is more than merely vengeance: it is premeditated murder and it taints not only its victim, but also his next of kin.*

"The real name of punishment that is inflicted without any melioristic intention is vengeance." What is capital punishment except a reply to blood with blood and a perennial recourse to the *lex talionis?* Even that barbarous law, in its own gross calculations, aspired to a kind of justice. But capital punishment exacts only a death "with suffering worse than death."

On the terrors of the prisoner in death's row, on his slow

disintegration in fear, and the pointlessness of his suffering, Camus has written five unforgettable pages which are objective without dryness, eloquent without bombast, and, quite simply, edifying. He concludes: "As a general rule, the prisoner is destroyed by his anticipation of death long before he actually dies. Though he himself has killed only once, he really dies twice, and the first death is worse than the second. Compared to such cruelty, even the *lex talionis* seems civilized. At least it never insisted that the man who blinded his brother had to lose both of his own eyes." (p. 153) And what, if anything, can be said for the parents of the condemned man, or for his kinsmen, who suffer so undeservedly from this injustice?

d) *The death sentence is absolute and irreparable, but the guilt it punishes is, of necessity, relative.*

No one is totally responsible, either for the good or for the evil that he does. In any event, a State such as France, which tolerates gin-mills and dives, and subsidizes "the sugar-beet at the expense of public housing," should surely ask, before passing sentence, in what way she has herself contributed to the crimes that she judges. Should not something be said then about the incomparable catalogue of crimes committed by alcoholics and the children of alcoholics? But the conscience of France is apparently easy, for she goes on chopping off the very heads that she helps drive insane, with no second thought about the relation between the punishment and the crime.

e) *Capital punishment does away with the criminal, but this really begs rather than solves the whole question of human evil.*

Capital punishment destroys the criminal and, with him,

every chance to amend a miscarriage of justice. It ties, in one remorseless knot, the quivering threads of chance, and, in passing sentence, sums up in a final, logical sentence the actual relativity of human affairs. Yet, except for certain "incorrigible monsters," criminals are only sorrier specimens of our common human weakness. "Even in error and evil, mankind is a community." (p. 164) We could wish, therefore, that the compassion that should temper human justice would keep this community in mind and do away with the "supreme penalty."

Here Camus interrupts his argument to ask this question:

"What does the death penalty actually mean to the men of the middle of the Twentieth Century?"

His detailed answer constitutes, in our opinion, the most characteristic part of his exposition. By grounding the debate in the field of historical fact, the author aligns himself with the trend of thought that, from *The Plague* to *The Rebel*, and from *Les Justes* to *The Fall*, has crystallized around the theme of human and natural evil.

Both logic and fact, he says, demand the abolition of capital punishment:

By reason of logic:

In earlier times when the king, acting as God's earthly deputy, or the clergy pronounced the death penalty, they did not cut off the criminal from salvation. The punishment was provisional and it left the final judgment, which rested with God, in suspense. At the hour of his death, the condemned man could still repent and be saved. The Catholic Church could, on these grounds, consider capital punishment "as a powerful means of salvation." "Only religious values, particularly belief in an afterlife, can justify capital punishment since, according to their peculiar logic, they deny that it is absolute and irreparable. It is defensible because it is not final." (pp. 169-170)

But, in our secularized society, such a justification can scarcely be said to exist. "When a judge who is an atheist, or a skeptic, or an agnostic, passes the death penalty on an unbeliever, he pronounces a sentence beyond recall. He places himself on the throne of God, though his authority hardly rivals his ambition, and he would be the first to deny that this is what he is doing." (p. 172) Moreover, who of us can say in his heart that he is an absolute innocent, and so claim the right to set himself up as a supreme judge? "There are no just men, but only hearts that are more or less meanly just. For as long as we live, we are at least aware of this, and have the power to add to the sum of our actions some little good that may compensate in part for the evil that we sow through the world." (p. 168) The community of men in evil is strengthened by whatever mobilizes it against evil, and most of all, against death. Capital punishment, although it no longer has a religious sanction, yet militates against both the heavenly and earthly communities: against the heavenly, by presuming to judge that any man, however evil he may be, deserves no chance to be better; against the earthly, by adding to human evil a punishment that no transcendent reason can justify.

By reason of fact:

So many crimes have been, and are being, committed in the name of the modern State—it is not even necessary to include the wars that have ravaged, and will ravage, the earth—that today the tables have been turned: it is no longer society that must protect itself against the depredations of the individual, but the individual who must protect himself against the madness of a deified society that has become through the erosion of faith the object of its own devotion.

"To abolish capital punishment would constitute a public declaration that society and the State are not, in themselves, absolute values, and that they have no authority to legislate absolutely, or to do what cannot be undone." (p. 175) Such a move would rescue the individual from the rampages of the social monster that threatens him, and perhaps permit Europe to regain the poise that her drunken pride has compromised. "In the united Europe of tomorrow, in behalf of which I am speaking, the formal abolition of the death penalty should be the first article of the *Code européen* that all of us are hoping for." (p. 176)

On this final note Camus reaffirms and strengthens the reasoning that, since *The Plague,* and especially since *The Rebel,* he has been systematizing and defining with increasing clarity and precision. There are echoes here, even in the style, of the discourse of Tarrou on the problem of evil and of our need to counteract it as best we can with the little good that is in us; of the words of Clamance about the depth of the roots that this evil sinks into us and about the community in misery that unites the judge and the suppliant; of the voice of the Rebel as he denounces the philosophy of nihilism and our mechanistic civilization; and, finally, the accents of the man of the Mediterranean as he diagnoses the delirium that has seized Europe and, with modesty and hope, heralds a renaissance.

BIBLIOGRAPHY

I. The Works of Albert Camus

1. Novels, Essays, Dramas

1937 L'ENVERS ET L'ENDROIT, Essays, in Coll. Méditerranéennes, Algiers, Charlot, 1937. Jean-Jacques
Pauvert issued a limited edition of 100 copies.

1939 NOCES, Essays.
   a) First edition, Algiers, Charlot, 1939.
   b) New edition, Paris, Charlot, 1945.
   c) New edition, Paris, Gallimard, 1947.

1942 L'ETRANGER, Novel.
   a) First edition, Paris, Gallimard, 1942.
   b) New York, Pantheon Books, 1946.
   c) With 29 etchings by Mayo, Paris, Gallimard, 1946.
   d) Private edition of the Club du Meilleur Livre,
   Paris, January 1954.

LE MYTHE DE SISYPHE, Essay.

a) First edition, Coll. "Les Essais, XII," Paris, Gallimard, 1942.

b) New edition, Paris, Gallimard, 1945.

c) Enlarged edition, after the design of Mario Prassinos, Paris, Gallimard, 1953.

1944 LE MALENTENDU, a Play in Three Acts, and CALIGULA, a Play in Four Acts, Paris, Gallimard, 1944.

CALIGULA, a Play in Four Acts, in a new edition, Paris, Gallimard, 1946.

1945 LETTRES A UN AMI ALLEMAND, Essays.

a) First edition, Paris, Gallimard, 1945.

b) New edition, with a previously unpublished preface, Paris, Gallimard, 1948.

c) Lausanne, Marguerat, 1946.

REMARQUE SUR LA REVOLTE, Essay, in *Existence* (essays by A. Camus, E. Gilson, J. Grenier, etc.), Coll. "La Métaphysique," I, Paris, Gallimard, 1945.

1947 LA PESTE, a Novel.

a) First edition, Paris, Gallimard, 1947.

b) Collection pourpre, Paris, Gallimard, 1949.

c) With 12 water-colors by Edy Legrand, Coll. "Le Rayon d'Or," Paris, Gallimard, 1950.

d) Abridged and annotated by J.-A. G. Tans and J.-P. Van der Linden, Bibliothèque française *Paul Brand,* série jaune, I, Bussum, 1951.

e) Private edition of the Club du Meilleur Livre, Paris, January 1955. With a previously unpublished preface: *Exhortation aux médecins de la peste.* (See *Archives de la Peste*).

ARCHIVES DE LA PESTE, Cahiers de la Pléiade, April 1947.

PROMETHEE AUX ENFERS, Essay. Paris, Palimugre, 1947.

1948 L'ETAT DE SIEGE, a Spectacle in Three Parts, Paris, Gallimard, 1948.

L'EXIL D'HELENE, Essay, in *Permanence de la Grèce,* Paris, Editions des Cahiers du Sud, 1948. (See, L'ETE)

LES MEUTRIERS DELICATS, Essay, in *La Table Ronde,* January 1948. (See L'HOMME REVOLTE)

1949 LE MEURTRE ET L'ABSURDE, Essay, in *Empédocle,* no. 1, April 1949. (See L'HOMME REVOLTE).

1950 ACTUELLES, Chroniques (1944-1948), Paris, Gallimard, 1950.

LES JUSTES, a Play in Five Acts, Paris, Gallimard, 1950.

LE MINOTAURE ou LA HALTE D'ORAN, Essay, Paris, Charlot, 1950. (See L'ETE).

1951 NIETZSCHE ET LE NIHILISME, Essay, in *Les Temps Moderne,* August 1951. (See L'HOMME REVOLTE).

L'HOMME REVOLTE, Essay, Paris, Gallimard, 1951.

1953 ACTUELLES II, Chroniques (1948-1953), Paris, Gallimard, 1953.

RETOUR A TIPASA, in *Terrasses*, 1953. (See L'ETE).

1954 LA MER AU PLUS PRES, a Poetic Essay, in *La Nouvelle N.R.F.*, January 1954. (See L'ETE).

L'ETE, Essays *(Le Minotaure, Les Amandiers, Prométhée aux Enfers, L'Exil d'Hélène, L'Enigme, Retour à Tipasa, La Mer au plus près)*, Paris, Gallimard, 1954.

ART (one page), Essay, Paris-Brussels, Editions G.-M. Dutilleul, 1954.

1955 LA FEMME ADULTERE, a Short Story, Algiers, Edition de l'Empire, 1955. Lithographs by Clairin. (See L'EXIL ET LE ROYAUME).

1956 L'ESPRIT CONFUS, a Short Story, in *La Nouvelle N.R.F.*, June, 1956. (See L'EXIL ET LE ROYAUME).

LA CHUTE, a Novel. Paris, Gallimard, 1956.

1957 L'EXIL ET LE ROYAUME, Short Stories, Paris, Gallimard, 1957.

REFLEXIONS SUR LA GUILLOTINE, in Arthur Koestler-Albert Camus, *Réflexions sur la peine capitale*, Introduction and Appraisal by Jean Bloch-Michel, Paris, Colmann-Lévy, 1957. (See also *La Nouvelle N.R.F.*, nos. 54 and 55, June and July, 1957).

2. *New Versions and Adaptations*

1953 Pedro CALDERON DE LA BARCA, *La Dévotion à la Croix*, a Play in Three Days, French text by Albert Camus, Paris, Gallimard, 1953.

Pierre de LARIVEY, *Les Esprits,* a Comedy, adapted by Albert Camus, Paris, Gallimard, 1953.

1955   Dino BUZZATI, *Un cas intéressant,* a Play in Two Parts and 11 Scenes, adapted by Albert Camus, performed at the Theatre La Bruyère by Georges Vitaly in March 1955. Published in *L'Avant-Scène,* No. 105.

1956   After William FAULKNER, *Requiem pour une nonne,* adapted by Albert Camus, Paris, Gallimard, Coll. "Le Manteau d'Arlequin," 1956.

1957   LOPE DE VEGA, *Le Chevalièr d'Olmedo,* French adaptation by Albert Camus, Paris, Gallimard, 1957.

3. Prefaces

1944   S. CHAMFORT, *Maximes et anecdotes,* preface by Albert Camus, biography of Ginguène, Coll. "Incidences," 2, Monaco, Dac, 1944.

1945   André SALVET, *Le Combat silencieux,* prefaced with a letter by Albert Camus, Paris, Le Portulan, 1945.

1946   Pierre-Eugène CLAIRIN, *Dix estampes originales,* presented by Albert Camus, Paris, Rombaldi, 1946.

1947   René LEYNAUD, *Poésies posthumes,* preface by Albert Camus, Paris, Gallimard, 1947.

Jacques MERY, *Laissez passer mon peuple,* preface by Albert Camus, Coll. "Esprit," Paris, Editions du Seuil, 1947. (See ACTUELLES II).

1951   Dr. Jeanne HEON-CANONNE, *Devant la mort,* preface in the form of a letter by Albert Camus, Algiers, Siraudeau, 1951. (See ACTUELLES II).

1952 Oscar WILDE, La Ballade de la Geöle de Reading, foreword by Albert Camus: "L'Artiste en prison." (Sections appeared in *Arts*).

1953 Alfred ROSMER, *Moscou au temps de Lénine*, preface by Albert Camus, 1953. (See ACTUELLES II).

Louis GUILLOUX, *La Maison du peuple*, followed by *Compagnons*, foreword by Albert Camus, Paris, Grasset, 1953.

1955 Konrad BIEBER, *L'Allemagne vue par les ecrivains de la Résistance française*, preface by Albert Camus: "Le rufus de la haine." (See *Témoins*, Spring 1955).

Roger MARTIN DU GARD, *Oeuvres Complètes*, volume I, preface by Albert Camus: *Roger Martin du Gard*, Bibliothèque de la Pléiade, Paris, Gallimard, 1955. (See also *La Nouvelle N.R.F.* No. 34).

1957 William FAULKNER, *Requiem pour une nonne*, translated by Maurice-E. Coindreau, preface by Albert Camus, Coll. "Du Monde Entier," Paris, Gallimard, 1957.

4. Lectures*

1948 *Le témoin de la liberté*, lecture delivered at the Salle Pleyel to an International Meeting of writers.

L'incroyant et les chrétiens, a talk to the Dominicans of the Avenue Latour-Maubourg, Paris.

1952 *L'Espagne et la culture*, lecture delivered at the Salle Wagram.

* The first two lectures are reprinted in ACTUELLES, Chroniques 1944-1948; the last two in ACTUELLES II, Chroniques 1948-1953.

Bibliography

Le Pain et la Liberté, lecture delivered at the Bourse du Travail de Saint-Etienne.

5. Articles

Since the author has included most of his articles in the two volumes entitled ACTUELLES, it is not necessary to list them here in detail. But special notice must be given to the brilliant editorials that he contributed to *Combat* (reprinted in ACTUELLES, Chroniques 1944-1948), and to the famous *Lettre au Directeur des "Temps Modernes"* (reprinted in ACTUELLES, Chroniques 1948-1953). Of particular importance, too, is his *Lettre à Roland Barthes sur "La Peste",* which appeared in *Club,* the monthly review of the "Club du Meilleur Livre," Paris, February 1955; his *Lettre au sujet du "Parti pris" de Fr. Ponge* (dated 1943), which appeared in *La Nouvelle N.R.F.* No. 45, September 1956; and, finally, his *Réflexions sur la Guillotine,* which appeared in *La Nouvelle N.R.F.* Nos. 54 and 55, June and July 1957 (see The Works of Albert Camus above).

6. Interviews

Of the six or so interviews that are collected in the two volumes of ACTUELLES, the following are cited by R. Quilliot in *La Mer et les Prisons* as the most significant: the interviews dated 15 November 1945, *Nouvelles Littéraires;* December 1945, *Servir* (Lausanne); 10 May 1951, *Gazette des Lettres;* and 28 March 1954, *Gazette de Lausanne.* Mention must also be made of the most recent interview with the Nobel Prize laureate, *"Le pari de notre génération,"* in *"Demain,* no. 98, 24-30 October, 1957.

Bibliography

7. Recordings

Chez Festival, Long Playing Recording: Albert Camus (*Le Malentendu, L'Etranger, Les Amandiers*), with the author, Maria Casarès, Alain Cuny, and Serge Reggiani.

Chez Philipps, Long Playing Recording: Albert Camus (*Les Justes, L'Etat de Siège, Le Malentendu*), with the author, Maria Casarès, Dominique Blanchar, Michel Bouquet, and Serge Reggiani.

II. BOOKS AND ARTICLES IN FRENCH AND ITALIAN DEVOTED TO ALBERT CAMUS

(Articles which appeared between 1942 and 1949 are not cited, because they are already included in the work of Marguerite L. Drevet, *Bibliographiè de la Littérature française (1940-1949)*, Genève-Lille, 1954, pp. 116-118, which is a supplement to the Bibliographie of H. P. Thieme.)

R.-M. ALBÉRÈS, *Portrait de notre héros*, Essay on the Novel, Paris, Le Portulan, 1945. "Albert Camus et le mythe de Prométhée" in *La Révolte des écrivains d'aujourd'hui*, Paris, Corrêa, 1949. *L'Aventure intellectuelle du XXe siècle (1900-1950)*, Paris, La Nouvelle Edition, 1950. "Albert Camus ou la nostalgie de l'Eden" in *Les Hommes Traqués*, Essay, Paris, La Nouvelle Edition, 1953. *Bilan Littéraire du XXe siècle*, Paris, Aubier, 1956.

Francis AMBRIERE, *La Galerie dramatique* (1945-1948), "Le Théâtre en France depuis la Libération," Paris, Corrêa, 1949.

G. ANTONINI, "*Les Justes* di Albert Camus," in *La Fiera Letteraria*, 22 January 1950.

Roland BARTHES, "*L'Etranger, roman solaire*," in *Club* (monthly review of the "Club du Meilleur Livre"), April 1954. "*La Peste*, annales d'une épidémie ou roman de la solitude?", in *Club*, February 1955.

Rachel BESPALOFF, "Le monde du condamné à mort," in *Les Carrefours de Camus*, special issue of the review *Esprit*, January 1950.

Maurice BLANCHOT, "Le Mythe de Sisyphe," in *Faux Pas*, Paris, Gallimard, 1943.

Pierre BRODIN, *Présences Contemporaines—Littérature*, volume I, Paris, Nouvelles Editions Debresse, 1955. *Id.*, volume III, *Courants et Themes principaux de la Littérature Française contemporaine*, Paris, Nouvelles Ed. Debresse, 1957.

R. CANTONI, "L'uomo assurdo di Albert Camus," in *Studi filosofici*, January-April 1948; See *La coscienza inquieta*, Milano, Mondadori, 1949.

Maria CARRAZZOLO, "L'etica di Albert Camus," in *Humanitas*, V, 1950.

G. C. CASTELLO, "*I Giusti* di Albert Camus," in *Sipario*, May 1950.

CRITICUS, *Le Style au Microscope*, II, "Jeunes Gloires," Paris, Calmann-Lévy, 1951.

Bertrand D'ASTORG, *Aspects de la Littérature Européenne depuis 1945*, Paris, Ed. du Seuil, 1952. "L'homme engagé," in *Esprit*, October 1947.

Pierre NERAUD DE BOISDEFFRE, "Albert Camus ou l'expérience tragique," in *Etudes*, December 1950. Reprinted with additions in *Synthèses* (Brussels), December 1950. "Albert Camus," in *Métamorphoses de la Littérature*, volume II,

215

Paris, Alsatia 1951 (new edition revised and brought up to date, 1952).

Pierre NERAUD DE BOISDEFFRE, Etienne BORNE, R.-P. DUBARLE, "*L'Homme Révolté* de Camus," Debates, in *Psychologie Moderne et Réflexion Chrétienne*, Paris, Librairie Arthème Fayard, cahier no. 3, January 1953. (Based on a discussion at the Centre Catholique des Intellectuels).

Gérard DELEDALLE, L'existentiel, philosophies et littératures de l'existence, Paris, Lacoste, 1949.

Robert DE LUPPE, *Albert Camus*, Paris, Edition du Temps Présent, 1951. *Albert Camus*, Classiques du XXe siècle, Paris, Editions Universitaires, 1952.

J. DU ROSTRE, "Un Pascal sans Christ," in *Les Etudes*, 1948.

F. FEDERICI, *Introduzione al "Mito di Sisifo"*, trad. A. Borelli, Milano, Bompiani, 1947.

P. FOULQUIE, "De la révolte à la charité," in L'Ecole, Paris, March 1952.

André FRANKIN, "*L'Homme Révolté*, un plaidoyer pour la vie," in *Passages* (Liège), April-May 1952.

Gilbert GANNE, *Interviews impubliables*, Paris, ed. André Bonne.

F. GOOSENS, "Présentation de *La Peste* d' Albert Camus," in S. RENARD and J. GUERITTE, *Le chrétien devant le mal*, Saint-Paul, 1949.

Francis JEANSON, "Albert Camus ou l'âme révoltée," in *Les Temps Modernes*, May 1952. "Pour tout vour dire . . . ," in the August issue of the same review.

Robert KANTERS, "Moralistes et Prophètes," in *Des Ecrivains et des Hommes*, Paris, Julliard, 1952.

M. LAPARADE, *Réflexions sur quatre médecins de roman:*

essai de définition d'un humanisme médical contemporain, Bordeaux, Samie, 1948.

A. LA PENNA, "Albert Camus o la conversione degli indifferenti," in *Belfagor,* November 1950.

Marcel LAVILLE, "Homothétie," in the *Journal des Professeurs,* Paris, 23 June 1951. (Reply to the criticism of Criticus).

LIVRES DE FRANCE (Bull. d'inf. du dép. étr. Hachette), November 1951, devoted to Albert Camus. The issue includes: *Camus l'Africain,* by Jean-Pierre Vivet; *Une Macumba au Brésil,* by Albert Camus; *L'Homme Révolté,* by André Billy; and a Bibliography of the works of Albert Camus.

Claudine MERSCH, *Les Essais méditerranéens* d'Albert Camus, Memoire de Licence in Philosophy and Letters, University of Liège, 1955. (Manuscript).

Charles MOELLER, "Albert Camus ou l'honnêteté désespérée," in *Littérature du XXe siècle et Christianisme,* I, Silence de Dieu, Tournai, Casterman, July-August 1954.

Emmanuel MOUNIER, "Albert Camus ou l'appel des humiliés," in *Les Carrefours de Camus,* special issue of the review *Esprit,* January 1950. *L'Espoir des Désespérés,* Coll. "Esprit," Paris, Ed. du Seuil, 1953.

Maurice NADEAU, "Albert Camus et la tentation de la sainteté," in *Littérature présente,* Paris, Corrêa, 1952.

G. NATOLI, "Albert Camus o la lotta contro l'assurdo," in *La Fiera letteraria,* 18 September 1947. See *Scrittori francesi,* Florence, La Nuova Italia, 1950.

Louis NÈGRE, "Les éstapes d'Albert Camus," in the *Bulletin de l'Association Guillaume Budé,* October 1955.

N. NICOLAS, *La pensée existentielle d'Albert Camus*, Doctorate Thesis submitted to the Faculté de Grenoble, May 1955. (Cited by R. Quilliot).

Liano PETRONI, "Albert Camus, cratore di miti," in *Il Ponte*, Firenze, March 1950. "Le *Actuelles* di Albert Camus," in the *Rivista di Letterature moderne*, Florence, no. 2, new series, 1951.

Henri PERRUCHOT, *La Haine des Masques* (Montherlant, Camus, Shaw), Paris, *La Table Ronde*, 1955.

Gaëtan PICON, *Panorama de la nouvelle littérature française*, Paris, Point du Jour, 1949. "A propos de *L'Exil et le Royaume*" in *Le Mercure de France*, May 1957.

Robert POULET, *La Lanterne Magique*, Paris, Nouvelles Editions Debresse, 1956.

Roger QUILLIOT, *La Mer et les Prisons* (Essay on Albert Camus), Paris, Gallimard, 1956.

Paul ROSTENNE, "Un honnête homme: Albert Camus," in *La Revue Nouvelle*, Tournai, Casterman, March 1950. "Albert Camus, L'Homme Révolté," in the February issue of the same review. *La Foi des Athées* (Introduction à une vue chrétienne de l'Histoire), Coll. "Presences," Paris, Plon, 1953.

André ROUSSEAUX, "Albert Camus et la philosophie du bonheur," in *Littérature du XXe siècle* (third series), Paris, Albin Michel, 1949. "La morale d'Albert Camus," in *Le Figaro Littéraire*, 21 October 1950.

M. SAINT-CLAIR, *Galerie privée*, Paris, Gallimard, 1947.

Jean-Paul SARTRE, "Explication de l'Etranger," in *Situations I*, Paris, Gallimard, 1947; hard-cover edition published by Palimugre, January 1946. "Réponse à Albert Camus," in

Les Temps Modernes, August 1952.

Gilbert SIGAUX, "Avec Albert Camus," in the review *Preuves,* no. 35, January 1954.

Pierre-Henri SIMON, *L'Homme en procès* (Malraux, Sartre, Camus, Saint-Exupéry), Neuchâtel, Ed. de la Baconnière, 1950. *Les Témoins de l'Homme* (de Proust à Camus), Paris, A. Colin, 1951. "Albert Camus, du nihilisme à l'humanisme," in Histoire de la Littérature française au XXe siècle, volume 2 (1900-1950), Paris, A. Colin, 1956.

Philip THODY, "Albert Camus and *La Remarque sur la Révolté,*" in *French Studies,* October 1956.

Léon THORENS, *A la rencontre d'Albert Camus,* Coll. "A la rencontre de . . . ," Paris-Brussels-Paris, La Sixaine, 1946.

Alfred WILD, "La philosophie de l'absurde," in *Suisse contemporaine,* Lausanne, December 1945.

III. TRANSLATIONS

This is a listing of the countries where the specified works of Albert Camus have appeared in translation:

NOCES: Switzerland (Die Arche);

L'ETRANGER: England, U.S.A., Germany, Italy, Denmark, Sweden, Norway, Holland, Finland, Iceland, Argentina, Czechoslovakia, Poland, Hungary, Yugoslavia, Portugal, Japan;

LE MYTHE DE SISYPHE: England, U.S.A., Germany, Italy, Sweden, Denmark, Norway, Argentina;

Bibliography

CALIGULA—LE MALENTENDU: England, Germany, Italy, Denmark and Sweden (CALIGULA only), Argentina, U.S.A.;

LETTRES A UN AMI ALLEMAND: Italy, Japan;

LA PESTE: England, U.S.A., Germany, Austria, Italy, Sweden, Denmark, Norway, Finland, Holland, Argentina, Portugal, Yugoslavia, Japan, Israel;

L'ETAT DE SIEGE: Germany, Japan;

ACTUELLES I et II: Japan;

LES JUSTES: Japan;

L'HOMME REVOLTE: England, U.S.A., Germany, Italy, Sweden, Argentina, Japan;

L'ETE: Switzerland (Die Arche), Argentina, Japan.

IV. Articles in English Devoted to Albert Camus

1946 "Absurdiste," *New Yorker*, April 20.

Eric BENTLEY "Note on French Existentialism," (Includes a list of Camus' writings); *Books Abroad* 20, no. 3.

N. CHIAROMONTE, "Albert Camus," *New Republic*, April 29.

"Eternal Rock Pusher," *Newsweek*, April 15.

"Man in a Vacuum," *Time*, May 20.

Portrait, *Books Abroad* 20, no. 4.

Portrait, *Saturday Review of Literature*, May 18.

1947 B. R. LANG, "Two Books, Two Creeds: Andre Gide's *Theseus* and *The Stranger*, by Albert Camus," *Books Abroad*, 21, no. 4.

Portrait, *Theatre Arts*, March.

1948 Biographical Sketch, *Saturday Review of Literature*, July 31.

Victor BROMBERT, "Camus and the Novel of the 'Absurd,'" *Yale French Studies*, Summer.

"Camus the Classicist," *Newsweek*, August 2.

Chamfort, (Translated by L. Le Sage), *Sewanee Review*, January.

Anthony CURTIS, *New development in the French theatre*, London, Curtain Press.

George JAGGER, "Camus' LA PESTE," *Yale French Studies*, Summer.

Michael MOHRT, "Ethic and Poetry in the Work of Albert Camus," *Yale French Studies*, Summer.

Portrait, *Time*, August 16.

V. S. PRITCHETT, THE PLAGUE, (Review), *New Statesman and Nation*, August 21.

1949 "The Artist as Witness of Freedom," (Translated by B. Frechtman), *Commentary*, December.

Between Yes and No, (Short Story, translated by B. Frechtman), *Partisan Review*, November.

CALIGULA, (Criticism), *Illustrated London News*, March 26.

Walter A. STRAUSS, *Albert Camus' CALIGULA: ancient sources and modern parallels*, Cambridge, Harvard University

1950 N. CHIAROMONTE, "Paris Letter," *Partisan Review*, September.

"Exile in Gotham," *Americas*, May.

1951 Portrait, *Saturday Review of Literature*, January 13.

1952 "Art and Revolt," (Excerpted and translated by J. Frank), *Partisan Review*, May.

N. CHIAROMONTE, "Sartre versus Camus; a Political Quarrel," *Partisan Review*, November.

W. FOWLIE, "French Literary Scene," *Commonweal*, May 30.

K. LANSNER, "Albert Camus," *Kenyon Review*, 14, no. 4.

Richard SEAVER, "Revolt and Revolution," *Merlin*, vol. 1, no. 3, Winter 1952-53.

1953 J.-M. DOMENACH, "Camus-Sartre Debate: Rebellion vs. Revolution," *Nation*, March 7.

GENET, "Letter from Paris," *New Yorker*, May 30.

"*L'homme révolté*," *Review of Philosophy*, January.

R. WARNER, THE REBEL, (Review), *Spectator*, December 4.

"What a Writer Seeks," *Atlantic Monthly*, June.

1954 Michael HARRINGTON, "Ethics of a Rebellion," *Commonweal*, January 29.

"Hopeful Frenchman," *Newsweek*, September 20.

H. KOHN, "Man the Undoer," *Saturday Review of Literature*, February 13.

Portrait, *Life*, October 4.

1955 K. BIEBER, "Engagement as a Professional Risk," *Yale French Studies*, no. 16, Winter, 1955-56.

Waldo FRANK, "Life in the Face of Absurdity," *New Republic*, September 19.

"How Good Without God," *Time*, October 3.

S. JOHN, "Image and Symbol in the Work of Albert Camus," *French Studies*, Oxford, January.

J. KORG, "Cult of Absurdity," *Nation*, December 10.

"The Writer and His Times," (Translated by Justin O'Brien), *Partisan Review*, Summer.

1956 John CRUICKSHANK, "Camus's Technique in L'ETRANGER," *French Studies*, Oxford, July.

Leslie A. FIEDLER, "Pope and the Prophet," *Commentary*, February.

H. R. GARVIN, "Camus and the American Novel," *Comparative Literature*, Summer.

T. L. HANNA, "Albert Camus and the Christian Faith," *Journal of Religion*, October.

P. THODY, "Albert Camus," *Contemporary Review*, December.

C. A. VIGGIANI, "Camus' L'ETRANGER," *Publications of the Modern Language Association of America*, 71: 865-87, December.

1957 L. ABEL, "Man Without Grace," *Commentary*, May.

J. D. BOYD, "No Man an Island?" *America*, March 23.

Edmund EGAN, "The Situation is Sin," (Review of THE FALL), *Catholic Worker*, vol. 23, no. 10, May.

H. GOLDBERG, "Violence of Virtue," *Nation*, March 30.

I. HAMILTON, THE FALL, (Review), *Spectator*, February 22.

I. HOWE, "Weight of Days," *New Republic*, March 11. Discussion, March 25.

Portrait, *Saturday Review of Literature*, February 16.

Portrait, *Time*, February 18.

R. RUSSELL, "The Inferno of Albert Camus," *Reporter*, April 4.

Bibliography

Philip THODY, "A note on Camus and the American Novel," in *Comparative Literature*, vol. IX, no. 3, Summer.

NOTE

On Albert Camus, Nobel Prize Winner for Literature in 1957, see especially the article by Emile Henriot in *Le Monde* of 18 October; the article by Jules Roy and the report by André Bourin in *Les Nouvelles Littéraires* of 24 October; and the articles by Roger Martin Du Gard, François Mauriac, Jean Grenièr, René Char, J.-C. Brisville, Jean Senard, and André Alter in *Le Figaro Littéraire* of 26 October.